WINDOWS 7
CONTROL PANEL
For System Administrators

Copyrighted © 2013 **John Monyjok Maluth**

Discipleship Press

Website: www.discipleshippress.wordpress.com
Email: maluthabiel@gmail.com

~~*~~

P.O. Box 28448-00100, Nairobi, Kenya

ISBN: 9781728809441

Library of Congress Control Number: 2022908663

All rights reserved. No part of this book may be reproduced, stored in a retrieval system, or transmitted in any or by any means – electronic, mechanical, photocopying, recording, or otherwise-without prior permission in writing from the copyright holder except as provided by USA copyright law.

CONTENTS

CHAPTER 1: WHAT THE CONTROL PANEL IS AND HOW TO NAVIGATE IT 1

CHAPTER 2: SYSTEM AND SECURITY 22

CHAPTER 3: NETWORK AND INTERNET 51

CHAPTER 4: HARDWARE AND SOUND 77

CHAPTER 5: PROGRAMS 100

CHAPTER 6: USER ACCOUNTS AND FAMILY SAFETY 121

CHAPTER 7: APPEARANCE AND PERSONALIZATION 144

CHAPTER 8: CLOCK, REGION, AND LANGUAGE 168

CHAPTER 9: EASE OF ACCESS 195

CHAPTER 10: WRAP-UP AND NEXT STEPS 217

CHAPTER 1: WHAT THE CONTROL PANEL IS AND HOW TO NAVIGATE IT

WHAT THE CONTROL PANEL IS, AND WHY IT MATTERS

In Windows 7, the Control Panel is the main place where you change system settings. It is where you manage security options, user accounts, printers, network settings, and how your computer behaves day to day.

Think of the Control Panel as the "settings headquarters" of Windows 7.

When something stops working, many fixes start here:

- Your computer cannot connect to the internet.
- Sound is not working.
- A printer will not print.
- Windows updates fail.
- The screen text is too small.
- A program is not opening the right file type.
- A family member needs a safer user account.

If you learn Control Panel navigation early, you save time later. Instead of clicking randomly or searching online for every problem, you will know where to go, what to check first, and how to make changes safely.

This book is not about memorizing every option. It is about building a clear habit:

- Find the right area quickly.
- Make one safe change at a time.
- Test.
- Undo if needed.

That habit turns you into a confident user and a reliable helper for other people.

What you will learn in this chapter

By the end of Chapter 1, you should be able to:

- Explain what Control Panel does in Windows 7.
- Open Control Panel using several methods (Start menu, Search, Run, and shortcuts).
- Switch between the three Control Panel views.
- Understand when Category view helps and when icon views help more.
- Use a safety checklist before changing settings.
- Take simple notes so you can reverse changes without stress.

How Control Panel is organized

Windows 7 Control Panel contains many tools, but they are grouped in a few main ways.

You will see one of these views:

1. Category view
2. Large icons view
3. Small icons view

Each view shows the same system tools, but the layout changes how you find them.

The biggest beginner mistake is not realizing the view changed.

A common situation looks like this:

- You follow steps from a guide.
- The guide says, "Click Network and Internet."
- But you do not see "Network and Internet."
- You think something is wrong with your computer.

Most of the time, nothing is wrong. Your Control Panel is simply in icon view, not Category view.

So the first skill is knowing what view you are using.

How to open Control Panel

There are multiple ways to open Control Panel in Windows 7. You should learn at least three. That way, if one method is not available, you still have options.

Method 1: Open Control Panel from the Start menu

1. Click the Start button (bottom-left corner of the screen).
2. Look on the right side of the Start menu.
3. Click Control Panel.

This is the most common method for beginners.

Tip: If you do not see Control Panel on the right side, your Start menu may be customized. Use the Search method below.

Method 2: Open Control Panel using Start menu Search

1. Click the Start button.
2. Click inside the search box at the bottom of the Start menu.
3. Type: control panel
4. Press Enter.

Windows 7 will show Control Panel in the search results.

This is one of the fastest methods once you get used to it.

Method 3: Open Control Panel using the Run box (keyboard shortcut)

This method is excellent when you want speed, or when you are helping someone and do not want to dig through menus.

1. Press the Windows key + R.
2. The Run box opens.
3. Type: control
4. Press Enter.

Control Panel opens immediately.

If you remember only one keyboard method, remember this one.

Method 4: Open Control Panel from Computer (useful shortcut)

1. Click Start.
2. Click Computer.
3. Look at the top area of the window for the address bar and toolbar.
4. Click "Control Panel" if it is visible, or use the navigation links.

Not every Computer window shows a direct Control Panel button, but many do.

Method 5: Create a desktop shortcut (optional, but helpful for beginners)

If you use Control Panel often, adding a shortcut saves time.

1. Right-click an empty area on the desktop.

2. Click New.

3. Click Shortcut.

4. In the location box, type: control

5. Click Next.

6. Name it: Control Panel

7. Click Finish.

Now you can open Control Panel from the desktop in one click.

Method 6: Pin Control Panel to the taskbar (optional)

This can make Control Panel available at all times.

1. Open Control Panel using any method above.

2. When Control Panel opens, look at the taskbar.

3. Right-click the Control Panel icon on the taskbar.

4. Click Pin this program to taskbar.

From now on, you can open it with one click.

Note: Some Windows 7 setups behave slightly differently, but the option is commonly available.

The three Control Panel views (and when to use each)

When Control Panel opens, look at the top-right area. You will see "View by:" with a dropdown.

That dropdown controls what you see.

View 1: Category view

Category view groups settings into big topics. This view is best when you are new and want a guided path.

Common categories include:

- System and Security
- Network and Internet
- Hardware and Sound
- Programs
- User Accounts and Family Safety
- Appearance and Personalization
- Clock, Language, and Region
- Ease of Access

In Category view, you often click a category first, then choose a smaller option.

When Category view helps:

- You are not sure where something belongs.
- You prefer a simple starting point.

- You are learning the general map of Windows 7 settings.
- You want fewer choices on screen at once.

When Category view can slow you down:

- You already know the exact tool you want.
- You keep clicking through multiple layers to reach a specific applet.
- A guide tells you to open a specific item that is easier in icon view.

View 2: Large icons view

Large icons view shows a long list of Control Panel tools as big icons. It removes categories.

This view is best when you want to go directly to a specific tool.

Examples of tools you might see:

- Device Manager
- Network and Sharing Center
- Programs and Features
- User Accounts
- Windows Firewall
- Power Options
- Backup and Restore
- System

When Large icons view helps:

- You know what tool name you are looking for.
- You want to scan visually with bigger icons.
- You are assisting someone and want them to find the icon easily.

When Large icons view can be annoying:

- The list is long.
- Beginners may not know which icon to pick.

View 3: Small icons view

Small icons view is similar to Large icons, but icons are smaller and more items fit on the screen.

When Small icons view helps:

- You are comfortable with Control Panel.
- You want speed and a compact list.
- You are following guides that mention specific Control Panel tools.

For beginners, Large icons view is usually friendlier than Small icons view.

How to switch views step by step

1. Open Control Panel.
2. Look at the top-right corner.

3. Find "View by:"
4. Click the dropdown.
5. Choose one of:
    - Category
    - Large icons
    - Small icons

Practice switching views right now. Do it slowly. Watch how the Control Panel page changes.

Important habit: If you are stuck, check the view first.

Navigating inside Control Panel pages

Control Panel is full of links, buttons, and side menus. You need to know three navigation tools:

1. The Back button
2. The address bar (breadcrumbs)
3. Control Panel Home

Using the Back button

The Back button works like a web browser.

- If you click into a setting page and want to return, click Back.
- If you clicked the wrong item, Back saves time.

Using the address bar (breadcrumbs)

At the top of many Control Panel pages, you will see a navigation path such as:

Control Panel > Network and Internet > Network and Sharing Center

Each part of that path is clickable.

- Click "Control Panel" to return to the main page.
- Click "Network and Internet" to go up one level.

This is one of the fastest ways to move around once you notice it.

Using Control Panel Home

In Category view, you will often see "Control Panel Home" on the left side.

If you get lost:

- Click Control Panel Home.
- You return to the main category screen.

Understanding links vs buttons: Apply, OK, Cancel

Inside settings windows, you will often see these buttons:

- OK
- Apply
- Cancel

Beginners often misunderstand them, so let's make them clear.

OK

- Saves the change.
- Closes the window.

Apply

- Saves the change.
- Keeps the window open.

Apply is useful when you want to test changes without closing the window.

Cancel

- Does not save changes made since you opened the window.
- Closes the window.

Important detail:
If you clicked Apply earlier, Cancel will not undo what you already applied. Cancel only stops changes that were not applied yet.

This is one reason the "one change at a time" habit matters.

The safety checklist before changing settings

This checklist is simple, but it prevents most beginner mistakes.

Use it before you change anything important.

Step 1: Confirm you are in the right place

Ask yourself:

- Am I in the right Control Panel view?
- Did I click the correct category or tool?

If you are following a guide and cannot find a menu item, your view is often the cause.

Step 2: Write down what you are about to change

You do not need fancy notes. Simple notes are enough.

Write:

- Date and time
- What you are changing
- The current setting
- The new setting

Example:

- Feb 3
- Power Options
- Current: Balanced, sleep after 30 minutes
- New: Balanced, sleep after 60 minutes

This makes reversal easy.

Step 3: Take a quick screenshot (optional but powerful)

A screenshot is often faster than writing.

To take a screenshot in Windows 7:

1. Press PrtScn (Print Screen) on the keyboard.
2. Open Paint (Start > type paint > Enter).
3. Press Ctrl + V to paste.
4. Save the file with a clear name like: ControlPanel_PowerOptions_Before.png

If you do not want to use Paint, you can also use the Snipping Tool in many Windows 7 editions:

- Start > type snipping tool > Enter

Screenshots are proof of what you had before. They reduce stress.

Step 4: Change one thing only

Do not change five settings at once.

If you do, and something breaks, you will not know which change caused it.

This rule is simple and strict:

One change.
Test.
Then the next change.

Step 5: Test immediately

After you change a setting, test the result right away.

Examples:

- If you changed the default browser, open a link and confirm.
- If you changed sound output, play a test sound.
- If you changed network sharing, try to access a shared folder.

Step 6: Know how to reverse the change

Before you click Apply or OK, take a second to locate the way back.

Look for:

- A "Restore defaults" button
- A dropdown where you can select the previous option
- A checkbox you can uncheck later

If you cannot see how to reverse a change, pause and read the options carefully before saving.

The "how to undo it" habit in practice

Undoing changes is not magic. In Control Panel, reversing a change usually means one of these:

1. Change the option back to the previous setting
2. Click "Restore defaults"

3. Use a restore point (for bigger system changes)

For most beginner tasks, option 1 and option 2 are enough.

Let's walk through a small example.

Example: You change the mouse pointer speed

1. Control Panel > Mouse
2. Pointer Options tab
3. You move the speed slider
4. You click Apply
5. You test by moving the mouse

Undo:

- Move the slider back to its previous position
- Click Apply again

The key is that you knew what it was before. That is why notes or screenshots matter.

Common beginner problems, and what to check first

Here are common frustrations that happen early. Use these checks before you assume something is broken.

Problem 1: "I can't find the menu item the guide mentions."

First checks:

- Check "View by:" and switch between Category and icon views.
- Use Control Panel Search (top-right search box inside Control Panel in many layouts).
- Make sure you are in the correct category.

Problem 2: "The button is greyed out, I can't click it."

First checks:

- You may need administrator rights.
- You may be using a standard user account.
- A work or school PC may block changes.

Try:

- Log in with an admin account (if you have permission).
- Right-click and use "Run as administrator" when available (mostly for tools outside Control Panel, but still a useful concept).

Problem 3: "I changed something and now I don't remember what it was."

This is why we use notes.

If you already forgot:

- Look for "Restore defaults."

- If it was a major change and you cannot fix it, consider System Restore (covered later in the book).

Do not panic. Most settings are reversible.

Practice tasks for Chapter 1

Do these tasks on a real Windows 7 computer or a Windows 7 virtual machine. These tasks are safe and help you build navigation muscle.

Practice Task 1: Open Control Panel using three different methods

1. Open Control Panel from the Start menu.
2. Close it.
3. Open Control Panel using Start menu Search.
4. Close it.
5. Open Control Panel using Windows key + R, type control, press Enter.

Goal: You should be able to open Control Panel quickly even if someone changes the Start menu layout.

Practice Task 2: Switch between views and confirm what changes

1. In Control Panel, switch to Category view.
2. Count how many main categories you see.
3. Switch to Large icons view.

4. Scroll and notice how many individual tools appear.

5. Switch to Small icons view.

Goal: Train your eyes to notice the view setting instantly.

Practice Task 3: Use "Control Panel Home" and breadcrumbs

1. In Category view, click Network and Internet.

2. Click Back to return.

3. Click Network and Internet again.

4. Click Control Panel Home on the left.

5. Click Network and Internet again.

6. Use the breadcrumb at the top to click Control Panel.

Goal: Learn at least two ways to escape a page quickly.

Practice Task 4: Create a simple change and undo it

Choose one safe change:

Option A: Change the Control Panel view and change it back.

- Switch to Small icons view.

- Write a note: "Changed view to Small icons."

- Switch back to Category view.
- Write a note: "Returned view to Category."

Option B: Change your system clock display format (only if you are comfortable).

- Go to Clock, Language, and Region.
- Explore date/time formats without saving changes.
- Cancel out and confirm nothing changed.

Goal: Build confidence that you can reverse changes.

Quick recap

- Control Panel is where Windows 7 settings live.
- You can open it through Start, Search, Run (Windows key + R), and shortcuts.
- The Control Panel view matters. Category view groups settings. Icon views list tools directly.
- If you cannot find something, check your Control Panel view first.
- Safety is a habit: write down what you change, make one change at a time, test, and know how to undo it.

Next chapter preview

In Chapter 2, you will enter the most important category for stability and safety: System and Security. You will learn how to read warnings calmly, handle Windows Update, understand Firewall basics, manage power settings, and build a simple recovery habit so you do not fear mistakes.

CHAPTER 2: SYSTEM AND SECURITY

WHY THIS CHAPTER MATTERS

If Chapter 1 taught you how to navigate the Control Panel, this chapter teaches you how to protect your computer and keep it stable.

Most serious Windows problems fall into one of these groups:

- Security problems (malware, unsafe settings, weak accounts)

- Update problems (missing updates, failed installs, restart loops)

- Stability problems (slow system, crashes, driver issues)

- Power problems (sleep issues, battery drain, overheating)

- Recovery problems (no backups, no restore point, no plan)

The **System and Security** category is where Windows 7 gathers the tools that reduce these risks. Beginners often avoid this area because it looks "technical." But learning it early is exactly what prevents panic later.

Your goal is not to become a deep system engineer overnight. Your goal is to become calm, careful, and consistent.

One safe step at a time. Test after each change. Know how to undo it.

What lives in System and Security

When you open **Control Panel** in **Category view**, you will see **System and Security** as the first major category on most Windows 7 systems.

This category usually includes:

- **Action Center**
- **Windows Firewall**
- **System**
- **Windows Update**
- **Power Options**
- **Backup and Restore**
- **Administrative Tools**

Depending on your Windows 7 edition and updates, you may also see items like:

- **BitLocker Drive Encryption** (common in Ultimate/Enterprise)
- **Credential Manager**
- **Storage Spaces** (not typical on Windows 7; more of a later Windows feature, but you may see related storage tools depending on updates and OEM utilities)

You do not need to master all of them at once. In this chapter we focus on the core tools that most users will need.

What kinds of problems this category solves

Here are real problems System and Security helps you solve:

- "Windows keeps warning me about something and I don't understand it."
- "A program cannot access the internet."
- "Updates keep failing."
- "My computer sleeps at the wrong time."
- "My laptop battery drains too fast."
- "I made a change and now the system is behaving strangely."
- "I lost my files and I have no backup."
- "The computer is slow and I don't know where to start."

This category is not only for emergencies. It is also for prevention.

If you set up good habits here, you reduce emergencies.

How to open System and Security

1. Open **Control Panel**.
2. Make sure "View by" is set to **Category**.
3. Click **System and Security**.

If you are in icon view:

1. Open **Control Panel**.

2. Look for the tools directly (Action Center, Windows Firewall, Windows Update, System, Power Options, Backup and Restore, Administrative Tools).

Action Center: Reading alerts without panic

What Action Center is

Action Center is Windows 7's warning and maintenance hub.

It collects important messages about:

- Security (firewall, antivirus, updates)
- Maintenance (backup status, troubleshooting reports)
- System health

The purpose is good, but the messages can feel scary to beginners. The key skill is learning how to read alerts calmly and decide what matters.

How to open Action Center

1. Control Panel
2. System and Security
3. **Action Center**

You may also access it from the small flag icon in the notification area (bottom-right of the screen), but Control Panel is the clearest path for learning.

Understanding the two main sections

In Action Center, you will usually see two main headings:

- **Security**
- **Maintenance**

Each section has a status:

- Green (good)
- Yellow (needs attention)
- Red (serious attention needed)

Do not panic when you see yellow or red. Read what Windows is actually asking you to do.

Common security alerts and what they mean

Here are common Security alerts:

1. **Windows Firewall is turned off**

- Meaning: your computer may be exposed to network risks.
- Safe response: turn it on, unless a trusted security tool manages it (rare for beginners).

2. **Virus protection is not found**

- Meaning: Windows does not detect antivirus software.
- Safe response: install a reputable antivirus if this is your personal machine. If it is a work PC, confirm policy first.

3. **Windows Update is turned off**

- Meaning: your system may miss security patches.

- Safe response: enable updates, or at least check for updates regularly.

4. **Spyware and unwanted software protection**

- Meaning: Windows is checking if protection tools exist.

- Safe response: confirm you have one trusted security solution, not many.

Common maintenance alerts and what they mean

1. **Backup has not been set up**

- Meaning: you have no reliable copy of your files.

- Safe response: set up Backup and Restore, or at least create a basic backup routine.

2. **Check for solutions to problem reports**

- Meaning: Windows has collected crash reports and may have fixes.

- Safe response: it is safe to check, but not urgent.

3. **Troubleshooting**

- Meaning: Windows troubleshooting can run automated checks.

- Safe response: use it as a starting point, not as the only solution.

A calm way to read Action Center

Use this simple approach:

1. Look at Security first.

2. If Firewall is off, fix that.

3. If Updates are off, fix that.

4. If antivirus is missing, fix that (if it is your personal PC).

5. Then look at Maintenance.

This order covers the biggest risk reducers.

"How to undo it" habit for Action Center

Most Action Center changes are reversible because you are usually toggling a setting on or off.

- If you turn Windows Update on, you can change it later.

- If you turn Firewall on, you can revert it later (but you usually should not).

- If you change maintenance messages, you can restore notification behavior.

Still, take notes whenever you change anything in Security.

Example note:

- Feb 3
- Action Center
- Turned on Windows Update
- Turned on Firewall

Windows Firewall: Basic protection and common fixes

What Windows Firewall does

Windows Firewall helps block unwanted network connections.

Think of it as a door guard:

- It can stop strangers on a network from reaching your computer.
- It can also block programs that try to connect out when they should not.

Firewall is not the same as antivirus. Firewall manages network access. Antivirus scans files and behavior. You want both.

How to open Windows Firewall

1. Control Panel
2. System and Security
3. **Windows Firewall**

The first thing to check: Is it on?

On the main Firewall page you will see:

- Firewall status for Home or Work networks
- Firewall status for Public networks

If it says "off," that is usually a problem.

Safe default for most people:

- Firewall ON

When a program "cannot connect" and the firewall may be involved

A common beginner situation is:

"I installed a program and it cannot connect."

Before blaming the firewall, check these first:

1. Is the computer connected to the internet?

- Check Network icon in the taskbar.
- Try opening a simple website.

2. Does the program have the right settings?

- Sometimes the program is misconfigured.

3. Is the firewall blocking it?

Allowing a program through the firewall

If you trust the program and need it to connect:

1. Open Windows Firewall.

2. Click **Allow a program or feature through Windows Firewall**.

3. Find the program in the list.

4. Check the appropriate boxes:

    o Home/Work (private) networks

    o Public networks

Safe beginner approach:

- Allow it on **Home/Work** only.

- Avoid allowing on **Public** unless you truly need it (public networks are higher risk).

If the program is not listed:

- Click **Allow another program…**

- Browse to the program file

- Add it carefully

If you are not sure, do not add it. Ask someone with more experience or verify the program is legitimate.

What not to do as a beginner

Avoid these two actions unless you clearly understand them:

- Turning Firewall off "just to test"

- Creating advanced inbound/outbound rules

Turning firewall off is like leaving the door open because you cannot find the key. It may solve a connection problem, but it creates bigger risk.

Better approach:

- Use "allow program" settings.
- Keep firewall on.

"How to undo it" habit for Firewall

If you allowed a program and later decide you should not have:

1. Go back to "Allow a program or feature…"
2. Uncheck the program
3. Or remove it

Write down:

- Which program you allowed
- Which network type you allowed it on

Windows Update: Patches, history, and failure patterns

What Windows Update is

Windows Update installs improvements and security fixes.

Updates matter because:

- They patch security holes.

- They improve stability.
- They sometimes fix drivers and compatibility issues.

In Windows 7, many problems happen when updates are disabled for long periods, then the system tries to catch up all at once.

How to open Windows Update

1. Control Panel
2. System and Security
3. **Windows Update**

Checking for updates

On the Windows Update page, you can:

- Check for updates
- See available updates
- See update history
- Change update settings

If you are on a slow connection, checking may take time, but do not interrupt it. Let it finish.

Understanding update types

Windows 7 updates often appear as:

- Important updates
- Recommended updates

- Optional updates

Beginner safe approach:

- Install Important updates first.
- Recommended updates can be installed if they are clearly useful.
- Optional updates should be reviewed carefully, especially drivers.

Changing update settings

Windows Update settings typically include options like:

- Install updates automatically (recommended)
- Download updates but let me choose whether to install
- Check for updates but let me choose whether to download and install
- Never check for updates (not recommended)

Best safe default for most personal users:

- Install updates automatically

If your internet is expensive or slow, you can choose a more manual option, but you must remember to check regularly.

Viewing update history

Update History shows:

- Which updates installed successfully
- Which updates failed
- Dates and error patterns

This is useful when:

- You suspect an update broke something.
- Windows keeps trying the same update repeatedly.
- You need to confirm if updates are happening at all.

Common update failure patterns (and what to do first)

1. Updates fail repeatedly with the same error
First steps:

- Restart the computer.
- Run Windows Update again.
- Make sure date and time are correct.
- Confirm you have enough disk space.

2. Updates stay stuck on "Checking for updates"
First steps:

- Be patient at first. Old Windows 7 systems can take long.
- Restart and try again.
- Check internet connection stability.

3. Updates install, but Windows keeps asking to install them again
First steps:

- Review Update History.

- Look for "failed" entries.

- If it is the same update, search for its code number later, but do not delete random files.

4. Updates cause slow boot or long "Configuring updates"
First steps:

- Do not power off during configuring unless it is truly frozen for many hours.

- Let it finish.

- After it boots, check Update History.

Your goal as a beginner is to do safe first checks, not advanced repair procedures. Later chapters can go deeper if needed.

"How to undo it" habit for Updates

Undoing updates is not always simple, but there are safe ways:

- You can uninstall certain updates (advanced, do carefully).

- You can use System Restore if a recent update caused trouble (we will cover the basics here).

At minimum:

- Record what happened.
- Record the date.
- Note whether the issue started after an update.

System basics: device name, system info, and protection

Opening System

1. Control Panel
2. System and Security
3. Click **System**

This page shows important information:

- Windows edition
- Processor (CPU)
- Installed memory (RAM)
- System type (32-bit or 64-bit)
- Computer name
- Workgroup/domain status

Why this page matters

This page helps you answer questions like:

- Can this computer run a certain program?
- Is it 32-bit or 64-bit?

- How much RAM does it have?
- What is this computer called on the network?
- Is it part of an office network?

When someone asks for "system specs," this is where you start.

Computer name

The computer name matters when:

- Sharing files on a network
- Connecting to the computer remotely
- Managing multiple computers

You do not need to change it often, but you should know where it is.

If you ever change it, make a note because it affects network discovery.

System Protection (restore points)

System Protection is your safety net for system changes.

A **restore point** is a snapshot of key system settings and system files. It helps you roll back changes if something goes wrong.

A restore point is not the same as a full backup. It usually does not restore your personal files like photos or documents. It focuses on system configuration.

How to open System Protection

1. Open System (Control Panel > System and Security > System)

2. Click **System protection** on the left

You will see:

- Available drives
- Protection status
- Create button
- System Restore button

Creating a restore point (safe and recommended)

Create a restore point before:

- Installing new software that changes system components
- Installing drivers
- Making major system setting changes

Steps:

1. Open System Protection.

2. Under Protection Settings, select your main system drive (usually C:).

3. Click **Create…**

4. Name it clearly: "Before changing power settings" or "Before installing printer driver"

5. Click Create.

6. Wait for confirmation.

This takes a few minutes.

Using System Restore (basic awareness)

System Restore can roll the system back to a restore point.

As a beginner, you should know it exists and how to launch it, but you should use it carefully and only when needed.

If a change caused a major issue:

- System Restore can help return stability.

We will go deeper later, but for now the key habit is:

Create restore points before risky changes.

Power Options: desktops, laptops, sleep, and hibernate

Power Options control how your computer uses electricity.

For desktops, this affects:

- Sleep timing
- Monitor turning off

- Energy use

For laptops, this affects all of the above plus:

- Battery life
- Heat
- How the laptop behaves when you close the lid

Opening Power Options

1. Control Panel
2. System and Security
3. Click **Power Options**

You will see power plans such as:

- Balanced
- Power saver
- High performance

Understanding common plans

1. Balanced
- Good default for most users.
- Mixes performance and power saving.
2. Power saver
- Saves energy and extends battery life.
- May reduce performance.

3. High performance

- Improves performance but uses more power.
- Can increase heat and reduce battery life on laptops.

Beginner safe default:

- Balanced

Sleep vs Hibernate (simple explanation)

Sleep:

- Saves your current work in memory.
- Uses a small amount of power.
- Wakes quickly.

Hibernate:

- Saves your current work to disk.
- Uses almost no power.
- Wakes slower.

For laptops:

- Sleep is convenient for short breaks.
- Hibernate is safer for long breaks because the battery will not drain as fast.

Changing when the computer sleeps (common beginner task)

1. In Power Options, pick the plan you use (usually Balanced).
2. Click **Change plan settings**.
3. Choose:
    - Turn off the display after
    - Put the computer to sleep after
4. Set times that make sense for you.
5. Click Save changes.

"How to undo it" habit for Power Options

Before changing times, write your current settings.

Example:

- Display off: 10 minutes
- Sleep: 30 minutes

If you do not like the result, restore them.

You can also restore default settings for a plan, but do not do it unless you are sure you want to reset all plan changes.

Backup and Restore: protecting your files

What Backup and Restore is

Backup and Restore helps you create copies of your files so you can recover them after:

- Hard drive failure

- Accidental deletion
- Malware damage
- System corruption

A restore point is not enough for file protection. You need backups.

Opening Backup and Restore

1. Control Panel
2. System and Security
3. Click **Backup and Restore**

What to back up (beginner priority list)

Start with what you cannot replace:

- Documents (school, work, writing)
- Photos and videos
- Financial files
- Projects and research
- Email exports (if important)
- Browser bookmarks (if not synced)

Do not assume your computer is safe forever. Hard drives fail without warning.

Where to store backups

Best options:

- External hard drive

- USB drive (for smaller backups)
- Network drive (if available)
- DVDs (older method, not ideal today)

Beginner safe advice:

- Use an external drive.
- Keep it unplugged when not backing up (reduces risk from malware and power surges).

Basic backup approach for beginners

- Set up a regular backup schedule.
- Use a dedicated external drive.
- Label the drive clearly.
- Test restore occasionally.

Even one good backup routine reduces stress dramatically.

"How to undo it" habit for Backup

Backup changes are usually not risky, but you should record:

- Where you are backing up
- What you selected
- How often it runs

That way, if something fails, you can troubleshoot quickly.

Administrative Tools: powerful tools, use carefully

Administrative Tools includes advanced utilities such as:

- Event Viewer
- Computer Management
- Services
- Task Scheduler
- Disk Management
- Local Security Policy (edition-dependent)

These tools are powerful. Beginners can easily change something without understanding it.

The correct beginner attitude is not fear. It is caution.

Why beginners should move carefully here

Administrative tools can:

- Disable important services
- Break login behavior
- Change system policies
- Affect storage partitions
- Affect startup processes

As a beginner, you can explore and learn what the tools are, but avoid making changes unless you are following a trusted process and you understand the reversal method.

Safe beginner approach:

- Open a tool to observe.
- Do not change settings.
- Close it.

Later, if you move into IT support, you will learn these tools step by step.

Practice tasks for Chapter 2

These practice tasks build your confidence in the System and Security category without risky changes.

Practice Task 1: Check Action Center status

1. Open Control Panel > System and Security > Action Center.
2. Look at Security status.
3. Look at Maintenance status.
4. Write down any warnings you see.
5. Do not "fix everything" if you are not sure. Just record what you see.

Goal: Learn to read alerts calmly and identify what is actually being requested.

Practice Task 2: Verify Windows Firewall is on

1. Open Windows Firewall.

2. Confirm it is On.

3. Click "Allow a program or feature…" and observe the list.

4. Do not change anything unless you understand it.

5. Close the window.

Goal: Learn where firewall settings live and how to check status.

Practice Task 3: Verify Windows Update settings and history

1. Open Windows Update.

2. Click "Change settings."

3. Write down the current update setting.

4. Go back and click "View update history."

5. Note if there are repeated failures.

Goal: Learn how to confirm if updates are working and how to find failure patterns.

Practice Task 4: Create a restore point

1. Open System.

2. Click System protection.

3. Click Create.

4. Name it clearly: "Chapter 2 practice restore point."

5. Create it.

Goal: Build the habit that prevents panic when a change causes trouble.

Practice Task 5: Choose a sensible power plan and adjust sleep time

1. Open Power Options.
2. Choose Balanced (if not already selected).
3. Change plan settings.
4. Adjust screen off and sleep times to sensible values.
5. Save changes.
6. Write down what you changed.

Goal: Learn to make safe daily-life changes while keeping the ability to reverse them.

Chapter recap

- System and Security is the stability and protection center of Windows 7.
- Action Center shows warnings, but you must read them calmly and prioritize Security first.
- Windows Firewall protects your network access and should usually stay on.
- Windows Update keeps your system patched and safer.

- System page helps you understand your computer and access System Protection.

- Restore points are a safety net for system changes.

- Power Options affects battery, sleep, and daily behavior.

- Backup and Restore protects your files, which matters more than most people realize.

- Administrative Tools are powerful and should be approached carefully.

Next chapter preview

In Chapter 3, you will learn Network and Internet, including how to read network status, fix common "no internet" problems, understand sharing, and avoid the mistakes that expose your computer on public networks.

CHAPTER 3: NETWORK AND INTERNET

WHY THIS CHAPTER MATTERS

Network problems are some of the most common Windows 7 problems.

People will tell you things like:

- "My internet is not working."
- "Wi-Fi shows connected, but nothing opens."
- "This computer cannot see the printer."
- "My shared folder disappeared."
- "It works at home, but not at the office."
- "It worked yesterday, now it does not."

Most of these issues can be diagnosed from one place:

Control Panel > Network and Internet

This chapter will teach you how to:

- Check your current connection status and understand what you are seeing.
- Identify the type of network you are on (Home, Work, Public) and why it matters.
- Use safe sharing defaults, depending on where you are.
- Understand HomeGroup, when it helps, and why it often causes confusion.

- Review Internet Options for basic privacy and security.

- Understand Remote Desktop basics and safe rules so you do not expose your computer.

Your goal is not to memorize every setting. Your goal is to build a reliable routine:

1. Confirm the network type and connection status

2. Test with simple steps

3. Change one setting only when you know why

4. Write down what you changed so you can reverse it

What lives in Network and Internet

In Windows 7 Control Panel (Category view), **Network and Internet** usually includes:

- **Network and Sharing Center**

- **HomeGroup**

- **Internet Options**

Depending on your edition and installed features, you may also see:

- **Connect to a network**

- **Set up a new connection or network**

- **View network computers and devices**

- **Proxy and LAN settings** (inside Internet Options)
- Some "remote" connection entries in certain setups

Even if your menu looks a little different, the big tool you will use most is:

Network and Sharing Center

What kinds of problems this category solves

Here are the typical problems Network and Internet helps with:

- No internet access
- "Limited access" or "No internet access" message
- Connected to Wi-Fi but cannot browse
- Wrong network type (Public instead of Home/Work)
- Network discovery is off, cannot see devices
- File and printer sharing not working
- Shared folder access denied
- HomeGroup confusion after password changes
- Browser privacy and security settings issues
- Proxy settings breaking the internet

- Unsafe sharing on public Wi-Fi

Let's start with the most important tool.

Network and Sharing Center

What Network and Sharing Center does

Network and Sharing Center is the main dashboard for network status and sharing in Windows 7.

It helps you answer basic questions fast:

- Am I connected to a network?
- Is it wired or wireless?
- Does Windows think I have internet access?
- What network type am I on (Home, Work, Public)?
- What sharing settings are enabled?

How to open Network and Sharing Center

1. Open **Control Panel**
2. Click **Network and Internet**
3. Click **Network and Sharing Center**

If you prefer icon view:

- Open **Control Panel**
- Click **Network and Sharing Center**

Reading the "View your active networks" area

When you open Network and Sharing Center, look for:

View your active networks

You will usually see:

- Network name (your Wi-Fi name or wired network label)
- Network type (Home network, Work network, Public network)
- Access type (Internet, No internet access, Local and Internet)

This section is the first place to look when someone says "internet is not working."

Network name

This might be:

- Your Wi-Fi name (also called SSID)
- "Network" (generic label on some wired setups)

Network type (very important)

Windows 7 uses network type to decide how open or locked your computer should be.

- **Home network**: sharing is easier, discovery is usually on
- **Work network**: similar to Home, but often managed more carefully

- **Public network**: safest and most locked down, discovery is usually off

Safe rule:

- Use **Public network** in cafes, airports, hotels, and anywhere you do not fully trust.
- Use **Home** or **Work** only in places you control.

Access type

This tells you what Windows thinks is happening:

- **Internet**: Windows believes it can reach the internet
- **No internet access**: connected to a network, but cannot reach the internet
- **Local only**: can talk to local devices, but not to the internet (some cases)

Sometimes Windows can be wrong, but it is still a strong clue.

Quick connection checks you can do from this screen

From Network and Sharing Center, you can click:

- The blue link next to "Connections" (for example: Wireless Network Connection)
- "Troubleshoot problems"
- "Change adapter settings"
- "Change advanced sharing settings"

We will use these in a safe order.

Diagnosing "No internet" without panic

When someone says "no internet," do not change settings immediately.

Start with a clean diagnostic routine.

Step 1: Confirm the obvious (fast checks)

Ask or check:

- Is the Wi-Fi icon showing connection bars?
- If wired, is the cable plugged in firmly?
- Is the router powered on?
- Is this a single-device problem or does every device in the room fail?

If every device is offline, the problem is likely:

- Router issue
- ISP issue
- Power issue

If only one computer is offline, the problem is likely:

- Wi-Fi password issue
- Adapter issue
- IP address issue

- Proxy issue
- Firewall or security software issue
- Misconfigured sharing or network type changes

Step 2: Confirm the network type

In Network and Sharing Center, confirm the network type:

- Home, Work, or Public

If you are on public Wi-Fi, Public is usually correct.

If you are on your home Wi-Fi and it shows Public, that can block sharing and discovery. Internet should still work, but sharing may not.

Step 3: Click the connection link and check status

In Network and Sharing Center, click the connection link next to "Connections," such as:

- Wireless Network Connection
- Local Area Connection

A status window opens.

Check:

- **IPv4 Connectivity** (it may show Internet or No internet access)
- **Media State** (if disconnected, cable or Wi-Fi problem)

- **Signal quality** (wireless)

Then click:

- **Details**

In Details, look for:

- IPv4 Address
- Default Gateway
- DNS Servers

Beginner-friendly interpretation:

- If IPv4 Address starts with **169.254.x.x**, the computer did not get an address from the router. This often means DHCP did not work.
- If Default Gateway is missing, the computer cannot find the router path.
- If DNS is missing or wrong, websites may not load even if you are connected.

You do not have to memorize these yet. Just learn to look.

Step 4: Use Troubleshoot (safe first tool)

From the status window, click:

- **Diagnose**

Or from Network and Sharing Center, click:

- **Troubleshoot problems**

Windows will run a guided check. Sometimes it fixes the issue. Sometimes it only reports the issue.

Either way, it gives you clues without you changing many settings manually.

Step 5: The restart order (simple but effective)

If troubleshooting does not fix it:

Restart in this order:

1. Disconnect and reconnect Wi-Fi (or unplug and replug the cable)

2. Restart the computer

3. Restart the router (only if you have access)

Many "no internet" problems are cleared by a clean restart.

Step 6: Check proxy settings (common hidden cause)

A proxy setting can break internet browsing, especially if it was enabled by:

- A work setup
- A VPN tool
- Malware
- A manual change

To check:

1. Control Panel

2. Network and Internet

3. **Internet Options**

4. Click the **Connections** tab

5. Click **LAN settings**

Look for:

- "Use a proxy server for your LAN"

Safe default for most home users:

- Proxy OFF

If you turn proxy off, test your browser again.

How to undo it:

- Write down what it was before you changed it.

- You can re-enable it if it was required in a work setup.

Important warning:

- If this is a work computer, proxy might be required. Ask before changing.

Sharing settings and safe defaults

Sharing is where many people accidentally expose their computer.

Windows 7 makes it easy to share files and printers, but you must know when it is safe.

The key idea: sharing depends on network type

Windows 7's sharing defaults are tied closely to the network type:

- Home or Work: sharing can be enabled safely in a trusted environment
- Public: sharing should usually be restricted

Opening Advanced sharing settings

1. Open **Network and Sharing Center**
2. Click **Change advanced sharing settings** (left side)

You will see profiles such as:

- Home or Work
- Public

Each profile has settings like:

- Network discovery
- File and printer sharing
- Public folder sharing
- Media streaming
- File sharing connections
- Password protected sharing

Do not enable everything. Use safe defaults.

Safe sharing defaults for home use

If this is your home network and you trust the people on it:

Recommended home defaults:

- **Network discovery**: ON
  Allows your computer to see others and be seen on the network.

- **File and printer sharing**: ON (only if you need it)
  If you never share files or printers, keep it OFF.

- **Public folder sharing**: OFF
  Public folder sharing can confuse beginners. Turn it on only if you understand it.

- **Media streaming**: OFF unless you use it
  Turn it on only for media devices you trust.

- **Password protected sharing**: ON
  This is safer. It requires a username and password to access shared resources.

Why password protected sharing matters:

- Without it, other devices might access shared files more easily.

- With it, you control access through user accounts.

Safe sharing defaults for office or school use

In many offices, IT controls these settings. If you have permission and must set them:

Recommended general office defaults:

- Network discovery: depends on policy
- File and printer sharing: ON only if required
- Public folder sharing: OFF
- Media streaming: OFF
- Password protected sharing: ON

If you are not sure, do not change these. Ask the admin.

Safe sharing defaults for public networks

Public networks include:

- Hotel Wi-Fi
- Airport Wi-Fi
- Cafe Wi-Fi
- Any network you do not control

Recommended public defaults:

- **Network discovery**: OFF
- **File and printer sharing**: OFF
- **Public folder sharing**: OFF
- **Media streaming**: OFF

- **Password protected sharing**: ON

If you are on a public network and these are ON, turn them OFF.

How to undo it:

- Write down what you changed and under which profile.
- You can turn them back on under Home/Work later.

The most common sharing mistake

Mistake:

- People turn on sharing while on a Public network because they want to share one file quickly.

Result:

- They forget to turn it off.
- Their laptop remains discoverable in risky places.

Better method:

- Use a USB drive for quick sharing.
- Or share temporarily on a trusted Home/Work network only.

HomeGroup basics

What HomeGroup is

HomeGroup is a Windows feature designed to make sharing easier between computers in the same home.

It is meant to simplify:

- Sharing libraries (Documents, Pictures, Music, Videos)
- Sharing printers

It uses a HomeGroup password and tries to reduce manual permissions work.

When HomeGroup helps

HomeGroup can be useful when:

- You have two or more Windows 7 computers at home
- You want simple file and printer sharing
- You do not want to manage usernames and permissions manually

Why HomeGroup often causes confusion

HomeGroup confuses many beginners because:

- It works best only in a true home setup
- It depends on network type being set to Home
- If one computer's settings change, others can lose access
- The HomeGroup password can be forgotten

- People expect it to behave like USB sharing, but it does not

Common symptoms:

- "I can see the HomeGroup but cannot access files."
- "It asks for a password I do not remember."
- "It worked, then stopped."

Safe guidance for beginners

If you do not need HomeGroup, you can skip it.

If you want to use it:

- Use it only on a trusted home network
- Keep password protected sharing in mind
- Write down the HomeGroup password
- Do not set up HomeGroup on public networks

Leaving and rejoining HomeGroup

If HomeGroup is broken, leaving and rejoining can help, but do not rush to do this.

Before changing HomeGroup membership:

1. Write down what computers are in the HomeGroup
2. Confirm the network type is Home

3. Confirm sharing settings are not disabled

If you leave a HomeGroup, shared access may stop until you rejoin and reselect what you share.

How to undo it:

- You can rejoin with the HomeGroup password, but only if you have it.

Internet Options: privacy and security basics

Internet Options affects how Windows handles internet behavior, especially for Internet Explorer, but parts of it also affect system-level networking.

This is where you adjust:

- Browser security levels
- Privacy settings
- Pop-up blocker behavior
- Certificates
- Connection settings, including proxy

How to open Internet Options

1. Control Panel
2. Network and Internet
3. **Internet Options**

Tabs you should know (beginner focus)

General tab

- Home page settings
- Browsing history
- Temporary files

Useful when:

- Browser is slow due to cached files
- You want to clear history on a shared PC

Do not over-clear if you need saved sessions, but clearing temporary files can improve performance on older systems.

Security tab

Windows uses security zones:

- Internet
- Local intranet
- Trusted sites
- Restricted sites

Beginner safe advice:

- Do not lower security levels without a strong reason.
- If a site demands unsafe settings, do not force it. It may be risky.

Privacy tab

Privacy settings control:

- Cookies handling
- Tracking behavior (limited in older browsers)

Beginner safe advice:

- Keep default settings unless you have a specific reason.
- If a site breaks, adjust carefully and then restore later.

Connections tab

This is important for internet problems.

It includes:

- Dial-up and VPN settings (if used)
- LAN settings (proxy)

If browsing is broken but the network shows connected, check proxy here as described earlier.

Advanced tab

This includes many technical settings.

Beginner safe advice:

- Avoid changing advanced settings unless you follow a trusted fix and you can undo it.

If you changed many settings and things became unstable, there is often a "Reset" option, but use it carefully because it affects browsing behavior broadly.

Remote Desktop basics (what it is and safe rules)

Remote Desktop is a tool that lets you connect to another computer and control it from afar.

There are two separate ideas:

1. **Remote Desktop Connection** (the client): your computer connects to another machine
2. **Remote Desktop hosting** (the host): your computer allows incoming Remote Desktop connections

Beginners often confuse them.

When Remote Desktop is useful

Remote Desktop is useful when:

- You need to manage an office computer remotely
- You need to help someone troubleshoot (in a controlled environment)
- You are working on a machine in another room

When you should avoid it

Avoid enabling Remote Desktop if:

- You do not fully understand who can connect
- The computer is on a public network

- You cannot control passwords and user accounts
- You do not have a strong reason

Remote access is powerful, and it can become a security risk if misused.

Safe rules for Remote Desktop

If you must use Remote Desktop:

- Use strong passwords on all accounts
- Allow access only to specific users
- Do not enable it on public networks
- Keep Windows Firewall on
- Prefer using it inside a trusted network, not across the open internet

Where to find Remote Desktop settings in Windows 7

Remote Desktop hosting settings are usually found here:

- Control Panel > System and Security > System > Remote settings

Remote Desktop Connection (the client) is commonly found here:

- Start > All Programs > Accessories > Remote Desktop Connection

In some setups, you may also see related remote connection entries under Network and Internet.

Do not worry if your menu differs. The safe rules stay the same.

Practice tasks for Chapter 3

These practice tasks focus on safe diagnosis and safe sharing. Do them on a real Windows 7 computer or a Windows 7 virtual machine.

Practice Task 1: Confirm your current network type

1. Open Network and Sharing Center.

2. Under "View your active networks," locate:

    o Network name

    o Network type (Home, Work, Public)

    o Access type

3. Write down what you see.

Goal: Train yourself to check network type first, before changing settings.

Practice Task 2: Diagnose "no internet" using the safe routine

Simulate the routine even if your internet works.

1. Open Network and Sharing Center.

2. Click your connection link (Wireless Network Connection or Local Area Connection).

3. Click Details.
4. Write down:
   - IPv4 Address
   - Default Gateway
   - DNS Servers
5. Click Diagnose and watch what Windows checks.
6. Close without changing anything.

Goal: Learn where key details live and build calm habits.

Practice Task 3: Review advanced sharing settings for each profile

1. Open Network and Sharing Center.
2. Click Change advanced sharing settings.
3. Expand "Home or Work" and write down:
   - Network discovery status
   - File and printer sharing status
   - Password protected sharing status
4. Expand "Public" and write down the same.
5. If Public profile shows discovery or sharing ON, turn them OFF and write it down.

Goal: Learn safe defaults and avoid accidental exposure on public networks.

Practice Task 4: Check proxy settings

1. Open Internet Options.
2. Go to Connections tab.
3. Click LAN settings.
4. Write down whether proxy is enabled.
5. If you change it, test browsing immediately and record the change.

Goal: Learn the hidden setting that breaks browsing for many users.

Practice Task 5: Find Remote Desktop settings without enabling anything

1. Open Control Panel > System and Security > System.
2. Click Remote settings.
3. Read the options but do not change them.
4. Close the window.

Goal: Learn where Remote Desktop lives and respect that it is a security-sensitive feature.

Chapter recap

- Network and Internet is where Windows 7 gathers tools for connectivity, sharing, and browser-related networking settings.

- Network and Sharing Center is your main dashboard for diagnosing problems.

- Always check network type (Home, Work, Public) because it affects sharing and discovery.

- Diagnose "no internet" with simple steps first: connection status, details, troubleshoot, restart order, then proxy checks.

- Use safe sharing defaults. Keep sharing OFF on public networks.

- HomeGroup can help in a simple home setup, but it often confuses users when passwords and network types change.

- Internet Options includes proxy settings that can silently break browsing.

- Remote Desktop is powerful and should be enabled only with strong passwords, trusted networks, and clear need.

Next chapter preview

In Chapter 4, you will learn **Hardware and Sound,** including Devices and Printers, safe AutoPlay settings, driver awareness for beginners, and the fastest way to solve common "no sound" and printer problems without guessing.

CHAPTER 4: HARDWARE AND SOUND

WHY THIS CHAPTER MATTERS

Hardware problems feel frustrating because you cannot "argue" with a printer, a speaker, or a USB drive. When a device fails, people often guess, unplug everything, reinstall random software, or panic.

But most Windows 7 hardware problems can be solved calmly if you follow a simple approach:

1. Confirm Windows can see the device

2. Confirm the device is powered and connected correctly

3. Use the right Control Panel tool to check status

4. Test with the simplest method (test page, test sound)

5. Only then think about drivers or reinstalling

The **Hardware and Sound** category is where Windows 7 gives you tools for:

- Printers and other devices

- AutoPlay behavior for USB drives and media

- Audio playback and recording settings

This chapter will teach you how to solve common issues without guessing, while keeping your computer safe.

What lives in Hardware and Sound

In Control Panel (Category view), **Hardware and Sound** usually includes:

- **Devices and Printers**
- **Device Manager** (sometimes shown as a link)
- **Sound**
- **AutoPlay**
- **Power Options** (also appears under System and Security)
- Other hardware-related tools depending on your PC

In this chapter, we focus on:

- Devices and Printers
- Printer setup and troubleshooting
- AutoPlay
- Sound settings and "no sound" fixes

What kinds of problems this category solves

Here are common problems you will solve using Hardware and Sound:

- "My printer is not printing."

- "The computer cannot find the printer."
- "The printer prints, but the output is blank or wrong."
- "The printer is offline."
- "I plugged in a USB drive, and something weird happened."
- "AutoPlay keeps popping up and annoying me."
- "A USB drive opens the wrong program."
- "My computer has no sound."
- "Sound comes from the wrong device."
- "My microphone is not working."

Let's start with the tool you will use most often here.

Devices and Printers

What Devices and Printers is

Devices and Printers is a Control Panel page that shows:

- Printers connected to your computer
- Other devices such as mice, keyboards, phones, and some Bluetooth devices
- The status of printers, including whether they are ready, offline, or have errors

This is one of the best places to start when you are working with printing problems.

How to open Devices and Printers

1. Open **Control Panel**

2. Click **Hardware and Sound**

3. Click **Devices and Printers**

You will see icons for devices. Printers usually appear in their own section.

Understanding printer status icons

Printers can show different status messages. Common ones include:

- **Ready**: printer is installed and available

- **Offline**: Windows cannot communicate with it right now

- **Paused**: printing is stopped by the user

- **Error**: there is a problem (paper jam, no paper, driver problem, or connection issue)

- **Default**: the printer with a green check mark (Windows uses it by default)

Do not try to fix everything at once. Start with the simplest cause.

Making a printer the default (common simple fix)

If a user prints and nothing happens, sometimes they are printing to the wrong printer.

To check:

1. Open Devices and Printers.
2. Look for the printer with the green check mark.
3. If the wrong printer is default:
    - Right-click the correct printer.
    - Click **Set as default printer**.

Test again.

How to undo it:

- Set the previous printer back as default.

Write down:

- Which printer you set as default.

Opening printer properties and preferences

Printers have two important menus:

1. **Printer properties**
2. **Printing preferences**

They sound similar but do different things.

Printer properties

This is more "system-level." It includes:

- Ports
- Sharing settings

- Driver info
- Test page button

Printing preferences

This is more "print-job-level." It includes:

- Paper size
- Print quality
- Color vs black-and-white
- Layout options

As a beginner troubleshooting printing, you usually start with **Printer properties**.

Printing a test page (the fastest real check)

A test page confirms three things:

- Windows can send a job to the printer
- The driver is installed and can communicate
- The printer can physically print

Steps:

1. Open Devices and Printers.
2. Right-click the printer.
3. Click **Printer properties**.
4. Click **Print Test Page**.

If it prints, the printer and driver are working. If your document still will not print, the problem may be:

- The program you are printing from
- A document issue
- The wrong printer selected
- Print queue stuck

If the test page does not print, continue troubleshooting below.

Printer setup (basic guide)

Before you install a printer, check the type

Printers can connect in different ways:

- USB printer (direct cable)
- Network printer (connected to router or shared through another PC)
- Wireless printer (Wi-Fi)
- Bluetooth printer (less common)

The installation steps and failures depend heavily on the type.

If you are not sure:

- Look at the printer cable or the printer screen.
- If it has a USB cable plugged into the PC, it is likely USB.

- If it connects to the router or has Wi-Fi, it is a network printer.

Adding a printer

Steps:

1. Open Devices and Printers.
2. Click **Add a printer** (top area).
3. Choose:
    - Add a local printer (often for USB)
    - Add a network, wireless or Bluetooth printer

Adding a USB printer (simple case)

Most USB printers are detected automatically.

Best practice:

1. Plug the printer in.
2. Turn it on.
3. Wait for Windows to detect it.
4. If Windows finds drivers, it installs them.

If Windows does not detect it, try:

- Different USB port
- Different USB cable
- Restart the printer and PC

Only after these do you consider manual driver install.

Adding a network printer (common in offices)

Network printers usually show up when Windows can detect them.

1. Choose "Add a network, wireless or Bluetooth printer."
2. Wait for the list.
3. Choose the printer.

If it does not appear:

- The printer may not be on the same network.
- Network discovery may be off.
- The printer may require manual IP entry.

As a beginner, do not rush into manual IP setup unless you know the printer's IP address and you have admin permission.

Printer troubleshooting: what to do before reinstalling

Beginners often jump straight to reinstalling. That is often the slowest solution.

Follow these steps first.

Step 1: Confirm power and paper

It sounds basic, but it solves many "printer not working" calls.

- Is the printer on?
- Does it show errors on its screen?
- Is there paper loaded?
- Is there a paper jam light?
- Is ink/toner low or empty?

Fix obvious printer-side issues first.

Step 2: Confirm connection

For USB printers:

- Check the USB cable is plugged in firmly at both ends.
- Try a different USB port.

For network printers:

- Confirm the computer is connected to the correct network.
- Confirm other computers can print.
- Check if the printer is connected to the router.

Step 3: Check if the printer is offline or paused

1. Open Devices and Printers.
2. Double-click the printer to open the print queue.
3. Click **Printer** menu at the top.

Look for:

- **Pause Printing** (should not be checked)
- **Use Printer Offline** (should not be checked)

If "Use Printer Offline" is checked:

- Click it to uncheck it.
- Try printing a test page again.

How to undo it:

- You can re-enable offline mode, but usually you do not want it.

Step 4: Clear stuck print jobs

If a print job is stuck, nothing else prints.

1. Open the print queue.
2. If jobs are stuck:
    - Right-click the job
    - Cancel
3. If jobs refuse to clear:
    - Restart the printer
    - Restart the computer
    - Try again

For most beginners, restarting clears many stuck queue problems.

Step 5: Print a test page again

After clearing issues, print a test page.

If the test page works:

- The printer is fine.
- The problem is likely the program or document.

If it fails:

- Now you can consider driver issues.

Basic driver care (beginner level)

What a driver is

A driver is software that lets Windows communicate with hardware.

When printers and devices misbehave, drivers are often involved, but drivers are not the first thing to change.

Why?
Because changing drivers incorrectly can create more problems.

When to suspect a driver issue

Suspect driver problems when:

- The printer installs but prints garbage characters
- The printer shows as installed but always errors

- A device is detected but does not work correctly
- A sound device appears but produces no output even when selected

Safe driver habits

Beginner safe habits:

- Do not install random drivers from unknown sites.
- Prefer drivers from the printer/device manufacturer.
- If Windows Update offers a stable driver, it is often safer than a mystery download.

If this is a workplace PC:

- Follow IT policy.

The "how to undo it" habit for drivers

Before installing or updating a driver:

- Create a restore point (System Protection)
- Write down:
    - Current driver name/version (if available)
    - The date you changed it
    - Where you got the new driver

That way, if something breaks, you can roll back.

AutoPlay: convenience and risk

What AutoPlay is

AutoPlay controls what Windows does when you insert:

- USB flash drives
- External hard drives
- CDs/DVDs
- Memory cards

For example, AutoPlay might:

- Open a folder to view files
- Ask what you want to do
- Automatically play music
- Launch an installer

AutoPlay is convenient, but it can be risky because removable media can carry malware.

A safer approach is to set AutoPlay to ask you what to do, or do nothing.

How to open AutoPlay

1. Control Panel
2. Hardware and Sound
3. **AutoPlay**

Why AutoPlay can be risky

AutoPlay can be used by malicious software to:

- Launch a harmful program automatically
- Trick you into running something you did not intend

Even if modern protections block many of these tricks, the safest habit is:

Do not auto-run unknown content.

Safer AutoPlay settings for beginners

Recommended safe default:

- Enable AutoPlay, but set it to **Ask me every time** for most media.

Or even safer:

- Turn AutoPlay off entirely for removable drives.

A balanced beginner setup is:

- For removable drives: Ask me every time
- For CDs/DVDs: Ask me every time
- For software and games: Ask me every time

The goal is control.

"How to undo it" habit for AutoPlay

If AutoPlay behavior becomes annoying or unsafe:

- Return to AutoPlay settings

- Change it back to Ask me every time
- Write down what you changed

Sound settings: fixing "no sound" the right way

Sound problems are extremely common, especially on laptops and PCs with multiple audio outputs.

A computer can have:

- Built-in speakers
- Headphone jack
- HDMI audio to a monitor/TV
- USB headset
- Bluetooth headset

Windows might send sound to the wrong device.

How to open Sound settings

1. Control Panel
2. Hardware and Sound
3. **Sound**

You will see tabs:

- Playback
- Recording
- Sounds
- Communications

For "no sound," start with **Playback**.

The most common cause of "no sound"

The wrong playback device is set as default.

Example:

- You plugged in an HDMI monitor once, and Windows switched audio to HDMI.

- Now your speakers produce no sound because Windows is sending sound to the monitor.

Fixing "no sound" step by step

Step 1: Check volume and mute (quick checks)

- Confirm the speaker icon is not muted.

- Confirm volume is not set to 0.

It sounds obvious, but it solves many cases.

Step 2: Open Playback devices

1. Open Sound settings.

2. Click the **Playback** tab.

You will see a list of devices such as:

- Speakers

- Headphones

- Digital Audio (HDMI)

- USB audio device

Step 3: Identify the correct device

Look for which device is:

- Plugged in
- Enabled
- Showing activity on its green level bar when sound plays

If you are not sure, play a test sound:

- Click a device
- Click **Configure** or **Test** (depending on what is available)

Step 4: Set the correct device as default

1. Click the correct device (Speakers or Headphones, usually).
2. Click **Set Default**.
3. Click OK.

Test sound again.

How to undo it:

- Set the previous device back as default.

Write down:

- Which device you set as default.

Step 5: Check if the device is disabled

Sometimes speakers are disabled.

In the Playback tab:

- Right-click in the empty area.
- Enable "Show Disabled Devices."

If you see a device disabled:

- Right-click it
- Enable

Then set it as default and test.

Step 6: Restart the audio device (basic)

If sound still fails:

- Disconnect and reconnect the headset
- Restart the computer
- Check again

Only after these steps do you start thinking about drivers.

Microphone and recording issues (basic)

If the microphone is not working, use the **Recording** tab.

Steps:

1. Control Panel > Hardware and Sound > Sound
2. Recording tab

3. Speak and see if the green bars move

4. If the correct mic is not default:
    - Select it
    - Set Default

If bars do not move:

- Mic may be muted, disabled, or the wrong device is selected
- Some laptops have a hardware mute switch or function key

Again, do not install drivers first. Check settings first.

Practice tasks for Chapter 4

These tasks train you to solve hardware and sound problems safely.

Practice Task 1: Set safe AutoPlay behavior

1. Open AutoPlay settings.
2. Set removable drives to "Ask me every time."
3. Save.
4. Write down what you changed.

Goal: Prevent automatic actions when inserting USB drives.

Practice Task 2: Printer test workflow (even if you do not have a printer)

If you have a printer:

1. Open Devices and Printers.
2. Identify the default printer.
3. Open Printer properties.
4. Print a test page.
5. Note the result.

If you do not have a printer:

1. Open Devices and Printers.
2. Observe what printers are listed (including virtual printers like XPS Document Writer if present).
3. Learn where Printer properties lives.

Goal: Know where to start and how to test quickly.

Practice Task 3: Correct audio output selection

1. Open Sound settings.
2. Go to Playback.
3. Identify what device is default.
4. Plug in headphones (if available) and observe if Windows changes default.
5. Set the correct device as default for your normal use.

6. Test with a sound (video or system sound).

Goal: Fix the most common "no sound" cause in under two minutes.

Practice Task 4: Take troubleshooting notes

Choose one of the following and write a small note log:

- Changed AutoPlay to Ask me every time.
- Set speakers as default playback device.
- Printed test page successfully.

Goal: Build the habit that makes undoing easy.

Chapter recap

- Hardware and Sound is where you manage devices, printers, AutoPlay, and audio.
- Devices and Printers is the first place to check printer status and print a test page.
- Troubleshoot printers with power, paper, connection, offline/paused, and print queue checks before reinstalling.
- Drivers matter, but they are not the first fix. Use safe driver habits and create restore points before changes.
- AutoPlay is convenient but can be risky. "Ask me every time" is a safe beginner default.

- Most "no sound" issues are caused by the wrong default playback device. Fix it in Sound settings first.
- Practice tasks build confidence: safe AutoPlay settings, test page workflow, and correct audio device selection.

CHAPTER 5: PROGRAMS

WHY THIS CHAPTER MATTERS

When people say "my computer is slow" or "something is wrong," very often the problem is connected to programs.

Examples:

- A program was installed and now the computer feels heavy.
- A program was uninstalled incorrectly and left problems behind.
- A program opens the wrong files.
- A program stops working after an update.
- A browser toolbar or unwanted add-on appears.
- Clicking a photo opens the wrong app.
- A PDF opens in the wrong reader.
- A file type icon changed and now a user is confused.

In Windows 7, Control Panel gathers program management under:

Control Panel > Programs

This area is the safe way to:

- Remove programs properly
- Repair programs when they support it

- Adjust default programs and file associations
- Manage optional Windows features (in many setups)
- Deal with Desktop Gadgets safely

If you learn this chapter well, you will avoid the most common beginner mistake:

Deleting program folders manually.

Deleting folders does not "uninstall." It often breaks Windows and leaves registry entries, services, and drivers behind.

This chapter teaches you to manage software cleanly.

What lives in Programs

In Control Panel (Category view), **Programs** usually includes:

- **Programs and Features**
- **Default Programs**
- **Desktop Gadgets** (on Windows 7)
- Sometimes "Turn Windows features on or off" (often listed within Programs and Features)

Different Windows 7 editions may show slightly different options, but these are the core.

What kinds of problems this category solves

Here are the common problems solved here:

- Removing unwanted software and toolbars
- Fixing a broken program install with repair
- Changing which app opens a file type
- Restoring correct file associations after installing a new app
- Cleaning up a shared computer without breaking essential software
- Managing older gadgets safely (or removing them)

Let's start with the main tool: Programs and Features.

Programs and Features

What Programs and Features does

Programs and Features shows a list of installed programs and lets you:

- Uninstall programs properly
- Change or repair programs (if supported)
- View installed updates (in many setups)
- Turn Windows features on or off (often linked)

This is where you go when you want to remove software the correct way.

How to open Programs and Features

1. Open **Control Panel**
2. Click **Programs**
3. Click **Programs and Features**

In icon view, you can click it directly.

Understanding the list

The list usually shows:

- Name of program
- Publisher
- Installed on date
- Size (not always accurate)
- Version

You can sort by clicking column headers. Sorting is very useful.

Useful sorting habits

1. Sort by "Installed On" when:
- The computer started having problems after a recent install.
- You want to find what changed recently.
2. Sort by "Name" when:
- You want to locate one specific program quickly.
3. Sort by "Publisher" when:

- You want to see all programs from one vendor.

Uninstall vs Change vs Repair

When you click a program, you may see one or more options at the top:

- Uninstall
- Change
- Repair

Not all programs support all options.

Uninstall

Removes the program.

Change

Modifies the install. For example, adding components or languages.

Repair

Attempts to fix missing or damaged program files.

Repair is useful when:

- The program crashes at launch.
- A program feature is missing.
- Files were deleted or corrupted.
- The program stops working after a system issue.

Repair is not available for all programs, but when it exists, it is often a safe first option before reinstalling.

The most important warning: what not to remove on shared computers

On a shared computer (office, school, family PC), uninstalling the wrong item can cause serious problems.

Beginners often uninstall something because:

- The name looks unfamiliar.
- They think it is "junk."
- They want to free space quickly.

But some programs are required for:

- Hardware drivers
- Printer functions
- Touchpad functions
- Graphics features
- Audio features
- VPN access
- Office tools

Here is a safe rule:

If you do not know what it is, do not remove it yet.

Types of items you should be careful with

1. Drivers and hardware tools
   These may include:

- Intel, AMD, NVIDIA graphics drivers
- Realtek audio
- Touchpad tools (Synaptics)
- Bluetooth tools
- Printer driver suites

Removing these can cause:

- No sound
- Low screen resolution
- No Wi-Fi
- Printer failure

2. Microsoft components
   Examples:

- Microsoft Visual C++ Redistributable packages
- Microsoft .NET Framework components

These are often required by other programs. Removing them can break multiple applications.

3. Security tools
   Examples:

- Antivirus

- Endpoint protection (work computers)
- VPN clients used for work

Removing them can violate policy or expose the system.

4. Office and productivity tools used by others
   On shared PCs, someone else may rely on certain software.

A safe removal checklist

Before uninstalling a program, ask:

1. Who uses this computer?
2. Do I recognize this program as essential?
3. Was it installed recently and linked to a problem?
4. Is it part of a driver or security package?
5. Do I have permission to remove it?

If you cannot answer, pause and research or ask.

Uninstalling a program safely (step by step)

1. Open Programs and Features.
2. Click the program once.
3. Read the program name carefully.
4. Confirm it is the correct program.

5. Click **Uninstall** (or right-click and choose Uninstall).

6. Follow the prompts.

After uninstall:

- Restart if asked.

- If not asked, restart only if the computer is behaving strangely or if the program was deep system software.

What if an uninstall fails?

Sometimes uninstall fails due to missing files or corrupted installers.

Safe beginner steps:

1. Restart the computer and try uninstall again.

2. If a Repair option exists, run Repair first, then uninstall.

3. If the program provides an official uninstall tool, use it.

Avoid:

- Downloading random "uninstaller" tools unless you trust the source.

- Deleting folders manually to "force" uninstall.

Repairing a program (when the option exists)

Steps:

1. Open Programs and Features.
2. Select the program.
3. Click **Repair** (if available).
4. Follow the prompts.

After repair:

- Open the program and test.
- If it still fails, you may need reinstall, but repair is a safe step to try first.

How to undo it:

- Repair does not usually harm anything, but you should still record that you ran it.

Write down:

- Date
- Program
- Repair attempt result

Turn Windows features on or off (basic awareness)

Many Windows 7 installations offer a link inside Programs and Features:

- Turn Windows features on or off

This controls optional Windows components, like:

- Internet Explorer components

- Windows Media features
- Some legacy services

Beginner warning: Do not turn off Windows features unless you know exactly why.

If you disable something incorrectly, other programs can fail.

Safe beginner use:

- Only view it so you know it exists.
- Leave it unchanged unless you are following a trusted reason and can undo it.

Undo habit:

- If you ever change it, record exactly what feature you toggled.

Default Programs

Why Default Programs matters

Default Programs controls what happens when you double-click a file.

Example:

- Double-click a photo (JPG) and it opens in a photo viewer.
- Double-click a PDF and it opens in a PDF reader.
- Double-click a music file and it opens in a music player.

Problems occur when:

- A new program takes over a file type.
- A user accidentally chooses the wrong default.
- A program is uninstalled but the association remains broken.
- A file opens with a program that cannot handle it.

This is a common beginner problem, and it is easy to fix once you know where to go.

How to open Default Programs

1. Control Panel
2. Programs
3. **Default Programs**

You will see options like:

- Set your default programs
- Associate a file type or protocol with a program
- Change AutoPlay settings (also found in Hardware and Sound)
- Set program access and computer defaults

The two most important for beginners are:

- Set your default programs

- Associate a file type or protocol with a program

Set your default programs

This option lets you:

- Choose a program
- Set it as the default for all file types it supports

Example:

- Set a certain browser as the default web browser.
- Set a certain media player as default.

Steps:

1. Click **Set your default programs**
2. Select a program from the list
3. Choose one of:
   - Set this program as default
   - Choose defaults for this program

"Choose defaults" is useful when you want the program to open some file types but not others.

Associate a file type with a program (file associations)

This is the best tool when one file type is wrong.

Example:

- .pdf opens in a browser when you want it to open in Adobe Reader.
- .jpg opens in a text editor because someone clicked "Always use this program."

Steps:

1. In Default Programs, click **Associate a file type or protocol with a program**
2. Wait for the list (it may take time)
3. Scroll and find the file extension (example: .pdf)
4. Click it once
5. Click **Change program**
6. Select the correct program
7. Click OK

Test by double-clicking a file of that type.

Choosing safe defaults

Safe default choices depend on what the user needs, but here are common beginner-safe choices:

- Photos: Windows Photo Viewer (simple and safe)
- PDFs: a trusted PDF reader (Adobe Reader is common on older systems)

- Web links: a modern browser available on the system
- Media: Windows Media Player or a trusted alternative

If the correct program is not listed:

- Click "Browse" and locate the program.
- Be careful not to pick random executables.

Undo habit:

- Write down the old default and new default.
- If the user dislikes the change, you can reverse it.

Desktop Gadgets (with a security warning)

What Desktop Gadgets are

Windows 7 includes Desktop Gadgets, small widgets like:

- Clock
- Weather
- Calendar
- CPU meter

They sit on the desktop and show quick information.

Why gadgets require caution

Desktop Gadgets have a history of security risk because gadgets can be abused.

The safest approach today is:

- Use gadgets only if you trust them fully.
- Avoid downloading gadgets from random websites.
- If you do not need gadgets, do not use them.

Many organizations disable gadgets entirely for safety.

How to manage Desktop Gadgets

1. Control Panel
2. Programs
3. **Desktop Gadgets**

You can:

- Add gadgets to desktop
- Remove gadgets
- Disable gadgets (depending on settings)

Safe habit:

- Use only built-in gadgets.
- Avoid third-party gadgets.

Undo habit:

- If you add a gadget, you can remove it from the desktop anytime.

- If a gadget causes trouble, remove it first before deeper troubleshooting.

Practice tasks for Chapter 5

These practice tasks are designed to be safe and useful. Do them on a personal Windows 7 system or a virtual machine. If you are on a work PC, follow policy.

Practice Task 1: Identify recently installed programs

1. Open Programs and Features.

2. Sort by "Installed On."

3. Write down the last five programs installed.

4. Ask yourself:

    o Do I recognize these?

    o Were any installed around the time a problem began?

Goal: Build the habit of using install dates to investigate problems.

Practice Task 2: Remove a test program (safe practice)

If you have a harmless test program you do not need:

1. Choose a small program you recognize.
2. Uninstall it using Programs and Features.
3. Restart if requested.
4. Confirm it is removed.

If you do not have a safe program to remove:

- Skip uninstalling and practice the steps without clicking Uninstall.
- The goal is to learn the process, not to damage your system.

Goal: Learn to uninstall properly without deleting folders manually.

Practice Task 3: Repair a program (only if the option exists)

1. Open Programs and Features.
2. Select a program that offers "Repair."
3. Run Repair.
4. Open the program and confirm it still works.

If no programs show Repair:

- Practice identifying which programs offer it.
- Write down at least one program that has Change or Repair.

Goal: Learn to use Repair as a safe first fix.

Practice Task 4: Fix a wrong default app for a common file type

Choose a common file type like:

- .jpg (pictures)
- .mp3 (music)
- .pdf (documents)

Steps:

1. Open Default Programs.
2. Click "Associate a file type or protocol with a program."
3. Find the file type.
4. Confirm which program is currently associated.
5. If it is wrong, change it to the correct one.
6. Test by double-clicking a file.

Goal: Learn to fix file associations calmly and quickly.

Practice Task 5: Review Desktop Gadgets and remove any you do not trust

1. Open Desktop Gadgets.
2. Review what is available.
3. If you see gadgets you do not use, remove or avoid adding them.

4. Do not download external gadgets.

Goal: Build a safe attitude toward gadgets and reduce risk.

Chapter recap

- Programs category is where you manage installed software and defaults safely.

- Programs and Features is the correct way to uninstall programs, not deleting folders.

- Be careful on shared computers. Do not remove drivers, Microsoft components, or security tools unless you are sure.

- Repair is a safe option when available and can fix broken programs without full reinstall.

- Default Programs fixes file associations and wrong default apps.

- Desktop Gadgets can be risky. Use only trusted built-in gadgets and avoid third-party downloads.

- Practice tasks focus on safe uninstall habits, repair workflow, and fixing file association problems.

Next chapter preview

In Chapter 6, you will learn User Accounts and Family Safety: how to create safer accounts, control admin rights, manage passwords, and set up basic protections on a shared computer without locking yourself out.

CHAPTER 6: USER ACCOUNTS AND FAMILY SAFETY

WHY THIS CHAPTER MATTERS

Many Windows 7 problems do not start with viruses or broken hardware. They start with people.

One person installs a toolbar. Another person clicks "Yes" on a prompt without reading.
A child plays with settings. A guest uses the same account as everyone else. Someone forgets a password and locks the family out.

User accounts are how Windows separates people, protects settings, and controls what changes are allowed. If you learn accounts early, you get three big benefits:

1. Better security
   You reduce the damage that malware and bad downloads can do.

2. Fewer accidents
   A standard user cannot easily change system-wide settings that break the computer.

3. Cleaner shared use
   Each person gets their own space, their own files, their own preferences, and their own limits.

This chapter will teach you how to build a safe, simple account setup that works at home, in small offices, and on shared computers.

What lives in User Accounts and Family Safety

In Control Panel (Category view), **User Accounts and Family Safety** usually includes:

- **User Accounts**
- **Parental Controls**
- Sometimes links related to credential management or user settings, depending on the edition and updates

In this chapter we focus on:

- User account types (Admin, Standard, Guest)
- Creating and managing accounts
- Passwords and safe account habits
- Parental Controls basics, including what it can and cannot do
- How to confirm who has admin rights

What kinds of problems this category solves

This category helps you solve problems like:

- "My child keeps changing things on the computer."
- "I need a separate account for work."

- "A program asks for admin permission and I don't know what that means."
- "Someone forgot the password."
- "Why did Windows ask me to confirm that change?"
- "A virus infected the computer because everyone uses the admin account."
- "I want limits on games or computer time."
- "I want to know which accounts are administrators."

Let's start with the basic idea that drives everything in this chapter.

The big idea: use the least power needed

Windows is safer when people do daily work in a standard account, and use an admin account only when necessary.

That is not about mistrusting people. It is about reducing damage from mistakes and malware.

If a standard account clicks something harmful, Windows blocks many system-level changes.

If an admin account clicks something harmful, Windows may allow it, and the whole computer can be affected.

So the safest everyday habit is:

- Browse, write, study, and use normal apps as a Standard user.
- Install software, manage system settings, and troubleshoot as an Admin only when needed.

Understanding account types in Windows 7

Administrator account

An Administrator account can:

- Install or remove software for all users
- Change system-wide settings
- Add or remove other user accounts
- Change security settings
- Access many protected areas of Windows

Admin is necessary for some tasks, but it is also risky in daily use.

Standard account

A Standard account can:

- Use installed programs
- Save files in the user's folders
- Change personal settings (desktop, some preferences)
- Use most hardware and network features

But a Standard account cannot easily:

- Install system-wide programs (without admin approval)
- Change system-wide security settings
- Modify protected system files

For daily use, Standard is the safer choice.

Guest account

The Guest account is meant for temporary use by someone who should not access your personal files.

Guest is limited, but it has drawbacks:

- It is often disabled by default
- It can create confusion on shared systems
- It is not always the best way to handle visitors

A safer modern habit is usually:

- Create a separate Standard account called "Guest" or "Visitor" with a password you control, then remove or disable it when not needed.

Still, you should know what the Guest account is, and where it lives.

When admin is needed

You do not need admin rights to do normal work. But you do need admin rights for tasks like:

- Installing new programs (especially system-wide installs)
- Installing drivers (printers, audio, graphics)
- Changing Windows Update settings
- Changing firewall settings
- Creating or removing user accounts
- Changing system protection settings
- Installing certain browsers, security tools, or office suites

A good pattern is:

- Keep one admin account for the person who manages the computer.
- Everyone else uses standard accounts.
- If someone needs to install something, the admin can approve it.

This is also how many offices manage PCs.

User Account Control (UAC): why Windows asks permission

In Windows 7, even admin accounts often see prompts that ask for confirmation before making system changes. This is called **User Account Control (UAC)**.

UAC prompts usually mean:

- "This action affects the whole computer, not just your files."

- "Windows wants you to confirm you meant to do this."

Beginners sometimes treat UAC prompts like pop-ups and click Yes without reading. That habit is dangerous.

Safe habit:

- Read the prompt.
- Confirm you started the action on purpose.
- If you did not start it, click No.

If you see prompts constantly from unknown programs, that is a warning sign. It can mean unwanted software is trying to make changes.

Opening User Accounts in Control Panel

1. Open Control Panel.
2. Click **User Accounts and Family Safety**.
3. Click **User Accounts**.

From here, you can do common tasks like:

- Change your password
- Manage another account (admin task)
- Change account type
- Turn UAC settings up or down (advanced, be cautious)

Creating accounts the right way

Why each person should have their own account

On shared computers, using one account for everyone creates these problems:

- Files get mixed up
- Browser history and saved passwords are shared
- One person's changes affect everyone
- Malware risk increases
- It becomes hard to know who changed what

Separate accounts fix most of that.

The best basic setup for a family or shared PC

A simple and safe setup looks like this:

- 1 Admin account for the computer owner or manager
- 1 Standard account for each adult user
- 1 Standard account for each child user with Parental Controls
- Optional: 1 Standard "Visitor" account if guests must use the PC

Steps to create a new user account

To create accounts, you must be using an admin account.

1. Open Control Panel.
2. Click User Accounts and Family Safety.
3. Click User Accounts.
4. Click **Manage another account**.
5. Click **Create a new account**.
6. Type the account name (example: "Mary" or "Kids").
7. Choose the account type:
    - Standard user (recommended for most people)
    - Administrator (use only for the main manager account)
8. Click **Create Account**.

After creating it, select the account and set a password.

Naming accounts clearly

Use names that make sense and stay consistent:

- John
- Mary
- Kids-James
- Kids-Sarah
- Visitor

Avoid unclear names like "User1" unless you truly do not care who uses it.

Switching users vs logging off

If more than one person uses the computer, learn the difference:

- **Switch user** keeps one person's programs open in the background.

- **Log off** closes that person's programs and signs them out.

Switch user can be convenient, but it uses more memory.

On older Windows 7 PCs with limited RAM, logging off is often better to keep the system fast.

Changing account types safely

Sometimes you need to change an account from Admin to Standard, or the other way around.

Safe rule:

- Keep at least one admin account you can access.

- Do not remove admin rights from the only admin account, or you can lock yourself out of system management.

Steps to change account type

1. Open Control Panel.

2. User Accounts and Family Safety.

3. User Accounts.

4. Manage another account.

5. Select the account.

6. Click **Change the account type**.

7. Choose Standard or Administrator.

8. Click **Change Account Type**.

Take notes before you change types.

"How to undo it" habit:

- Record the original account type.
- If something goes wrong, change it back using the admin account.

Passwords and basic account hygiene

Passwords protect accounts, but they also create support problems when people forget them. The goal is a balance:

- Strong enough to resist guessing
- Easy enough to remember without writing it on the monitor

Creating a strong, memorable password

A practical approach is a passphrase:

- A short sentence you can remember
- Mixed with numbers or symbols if needed

Example style (do not copy exactly):

- "MyDogRunsAt7!"
- "BlueRiver1984"

Avoid:

- "123456"
- "password"
- your name alone
- your phone number alone

Setting or changing a password

1. Open Control Panel.
2. User Accounts and Family Safety.
3. User Accounts.
4. Choose:
    - Change your password (for your own account), or
    - Manage another account (to change someone else's, admin only)
5. Follow the prompts.

If you are changing your own password, Windows will ask for your current password first.

If you are changing another person's password as admin, Windows may warn that changing it can affect access to encrypted files or stored credentials. On many home PCs, this is not a big issue, but the warning exists for a reason.

Password hints

Windows 7 allows a password hint. Be careful with hints.

Bad hint:

- "It's my birthday."

Better hint:

- "The river name + year."

A hint should help the owner remember, but not help strangers guess.

The password reset disk (important for home users)

Windows 7 offers a tool called a **password reset disk**. It is a USB or floppy disk that can reset your password if you forget it.

This is one of the smartest things you can do on a home computer.

Important:

- Create it right after setting a password.
- Store it safely. Anyone with that disk can reset your password.

Steps (typical path):

1. Open Control Panel.

2. User Accounts and Family Safety.

3. User Accounts.

4. Look for "Create a password reset disk" on the left.

5. Follow the wizard and choose a USB drive.

If you manage a family computer and people forget passwords often, this can save you from a full reinstall.

Account hygiene rules that prevent trouble

Use these habits:

1. One account per person
No sharing accounts for daily use.

2. Standard for daily work
Use admin only when needed.

3. Keep passwords private
Do not reuse the same password everywhere.

4. Lock the computer when you step away
Use Windows key + L to lock quickly.

5. Remove or disable unused accounts
Old accounts are risk. If someone no longer uses the PC, disable or delete the account after backing up their files.

6. Keep the Guest account disabled unless you truly need it
If you need a visitor option, a controlled Standard account is often easier to manage.

Parental Controls: basics, limits, and reality

Parental Controls in Windows 7 is designed to help parents control how a child uses the computer.

It can help with:

- Time limits
- Game restrictions
- Program restrictions (allow or block certain programs)

What it cannot do well by itself:

- Full internet filtering on all browsers (without extra tools)
- Controlling everything a clever child might try if they get admin access

The most important rule:

Parental Controls work best when the child uses a Standard account.

If a child has an admin account, Parental Controls become much easier to bypass.

Opening Parental Controls

1. Open Control Panel.
2. Click User Accounts and Family Safety.
3. Click **Parental Controls**.

You will see a list of accounts. Choose the child's Standard account.

Turning Parental Controls on

Select the child account, then choose:

- On, enforce current settings

From there, you can configure limits.

Time limits

Time limits let you choose when the child can use the computer.

You can block specific hours or allow only certain hours.

Example use:

- Allow computer time after school from 5 PM to 7 PM
- Block late night hours on school days
- Allow more time on weekends

This is very practical for families.

"How to undo it" habit:

- If you tighten limits, write it down.
- If the child needs extra time for homework, you can temporarily adjust and then restore.

Games restrictions

Windows 7 can manage games based on ratings, but how well it works depends on how games are installed and recognized.

You can:

- Block all games
- Allow games by rating
- Block specific games

For many families, the simplest option is:

- Block games during school nights
- Allow games on weekends

But you may prefer program limits instead, which is often more direct.

Program limits

Program limits let you control which programs a child can run.

This can be used for:

- Allowing only school apps, browser, and a few approved programs
- Blocking installers and system tools
- Preventing children from running certain games

This is one of the most useful Parental Controls tools.

Safe approach:

- Start by allowing common safe apps (browser, school software).

- Block anything that installs software or changes settings.

Warning:
If you block the wrong program, the child may not be able to do homework tasks. Make small changes and test.

Web filtering and Family Safety tools

Windows 7 Parental Controls alone does not provide strong web filtering across every browser. Microsoft offered additional Family Safety tools (often as part of Windows Live Essentials) that added web filtering and activity reporting.

If you need strong web control, you typically need:

- A trusted Family Safety tool

- Or a router-level filter

- Or a modern browser-based supervision tool

For this beginner book, the key is to understand:

- Windows 7 Parental Controls can manage time, games, and programs reliably.

- Web filtering usually needs additional tools.

Confirming which accounts have admin rights

Knowing who has admin rights is one of the best quick security checks on a Windows 7 PC.

Method 1: User Accounts screen

1. Open Control Panel.
2. User Accounts and Family Safety.
3. User Accounts.
4. Manage another account.

You will usually see each account with its type (Administrator or Standard).

Write down:

- Which accounts are admins
- Which accounts are standard

Safe rule:

- Keep admin accounts limited to trusted adult managers.

Method 2: Check your own account type quickly

In User Accounts, it usually shows your account name and type on the main page.

If it says Administrator, consider whether you really need that for daily use.

Practice tasks for Chapter 6

These tasks are designed to build real skill and safer habits. Do them on a personal PC or a

Windows 7 virtual machine. If this is a work PC, follow policy.

Practice Task 1: Create a Standard user account

1. Log into an admin account.
2. Open Control Panel > User Accounts and Family Safety > User Accounts.
3. Click Manage another account.
4. Create a new account named "TestUser" (or a real person's name).
5. Choose Standard user.
6. Set a password.

Test:

- Log off and sign into the new account.
- Confirm you can use basic programs.

Goal:
Learn the correct path for creating a standard account.

Practice Task 2: Confirm admin rights on the computer

1. Go back to the admin account.
2. Open Manage another account.
3. Write down which accounts are Administrator.

Goal:
Be able to answer, "Who can install software on this PC?"

Practice Task 3: Change a password safely

1. Choose a Standard account you control.

2. Change its password.

3. Log off.

4. Log in with the new password.

Goal:
Practice password change without locking anyone out.

Tip:
Write the password down temporarily in a safe place while practicing, then destroy the note after you memorize it.

Practice Task 4: Create a password reset disk (optional but strongly recommended)

1. On a personal PC, insert a USB flash drive.

2. Open User Accounts.

3. Create a password reset disk.

4. Label and store it safely.

Goal:
Prepare for the most common home emergency: forgotten passwords.

Practice Task 5: Set Parental Controls on a test child account

1. Create a Standard account named "ChildTest".
2. Open Parental Controls.
3. Turn Parental Controls on for that account.
4. Set a simple time limit (example: block late night hours).
5. Set program limits to allow only a few safe programs.

Test:

- Log in as ChildTest and confirm limits behave as expected.

Goal:
Learn how limits work and how easy it is to tighten or relax them.

Quick recap

- Windows accounts separate people and protect the system.
- Use Standard accounts for daily work. Use Admin only when needed.
- UAC prompts are not noise. Read them and confirm you meant the change.
- Create one clear admin manager account, and keep admin rights limited.

- Passwords should be strong but memorable. Consider a password reset disk for home use.

- Parental Controls work best for Standard child accounts and can manage time, games, and programs.

- Always test changes and keep notes so you can reverse them.

Next chapter preview

In Chapter 7, you will learn **Appearance and Personalization**, including taskbar and Start menu settings for daily productivity, display settings for comfort and readability, and Folder Options habits like showing file extensions so you can avoid common file and malware tricks.

CHAPTER 7: APPEARANCE AND PERSONALIZATION

WHY THIS CHAPTER MATTERS

When beginners hear "Appearance and Personalization," they often think it is only about making the desktop look nice. But in Windows 7, this category affects more than beauty. It affects comfort, speed, safety, and how easily you can find your work.

This chapter helps you solve problems like:

- "My screen text is too small to read."
- "Everything looks blurry."
- "My screen is stretched or the resolution is wrong."
- "My desktop is messy and I can't find anything."
- "My taskbar is full of icons and I don't know what matters."
- "Icons keep popping up near the clock."
- "A file disappeared, but I know it is there."
- "A file looks like a document, but it is actually a program."
- "I downloaded a font and now my computer acts strange."

Appearance and Personalization is where you learn daily habits that make Windows 7 easier to live with.

The single most important safety habit in this chapter is this:

Show file extensions.

That one change prevents many beginner mistakes and helps you spot risky files.

What lives in Appearance and Personalization

In Control Panel (Category view), **Appearance and Personalization** usually includes:

- **Personalization** (themes, desktop background, sounds, screen saver)
- **Taskbar and Start Menu**
- **Folder Options** (sometimes listed as "Folder Options" or "Show hidden files and folders")
- **Display** (text size, screen resolution, color calibration in some setups)
- **Fonts**

Your version of Windows 7 and installed features may add or remove a few items, but these are the core tools.

This chapter covers each one in a practical way.

Themes and desktop basics

What "Personalization" controls

Personalization controls:

- Desktop background (wallpaper)
- Themes (a set of wallpaper, colors, sounds, and screen saver)
- Window colors
- Sounds
- Screen saver

For beginners, the value is not only style. It is also:

- Making the screen comfortable for your eyes
- Reducing distractions
- Keeping a clean layout that improves productivity

Opening Personalization

1. Open Control Panel.
2. Click Appearance and Personalization.
3. Click **Personalization**.

A shortcut method:

- Right-click the desktop and choose **Personalize**.

Understanding themes

A theme is a package of settings that changes:

- Background
- Colors
- Sounds
- Screen saver

Windows 7 includes built-in themes such as:

- Windows 7
- Architecture
- Characters
- Landscapes
- Nature

You can click any theme to apply it.

Safe note:
Themes are generally safe, but be cautious with themes downloaded from unknown sources. Most problems come from third-party downloads and bundled installers, not from Windows themes.

Desktop background basics

You can choose:

- A single picture
- A slideshow (if supported)
- A solid color

For older or slower computers, a simple background can feel smoother. Heavy slideshows and high-resolution wallpapers can sometimes slow weak machines.

This is not always dramatic, but on low-memory systems, every little bit helps.

Window color and readability

Windows 7 allows you to change window color and transparency.

If you want clarity:

- Reduce transparency
- Use high-contrast colors
- Choose a theme that makes text easy to see

Your eyes matter. If you spend hours on a computer, choose settings that reduce strain.

Sounds and screen savers (practical use)

Sounds:

- You can change system sounds or mute them.
- If your computer is in a quiet office, reducing sound alerts helps.

Screen saver:

- Many people use it out of habit.
- Screen savers are less necessary on modern displays, but they can still be used for:

- Simple screen locking habits
- Visual preference

Important:
Screen saver is not a security lock by itself unless you require a password on resume. If you want security, lock your screen using Windows key + L.

Taskbar and Start Menu: daily productivity settings

The Taskbar and Start Menu are your daily control surface. Small changes here can reduce confusion and save time.

Opening Taskbar and Start Menu settings

1. Control Panel
2. Appearance and Personalization
3. Click **Taskbar and Start Menu**

Shortcut:

- Right-click the taskbar and choose **Properties**.

Understanding the taskbar

The taskbar includes:

- Start button
- Pinned programs
- Open program windows

- Notification area (system tray) near the clock

Beginners often suffer from a taskbar that becomes crowded, messy, and distracting.

Your goal is a clean taskbar with:

- A few pinned essentials
- Clear labels when needed
- Minimal noise near the clock

Key taskbar settings (and what they do)

Taskbar buttons: Always combine, hide labels vs combine when full

This setting controls how Windows groups open windows.

Options often include:

- Always combine, hide labels
- Combine when taskbar is full
- Never combine

Beginner-friendly choice depends on how you work:

1. Always combine, hide labels

- Windows groups windows from the same program into one icon.
- Clean look.

- But beginners can get confused because they cannot see file names.

2. Combine when taskbar is full

- Labels show until space runs out.
- Good balance for many users.

3. Never combine

- Every window shows separately with labels.
- Clear, but can crowd the taskbar quickly.

If you are a beginner and get lost switching between documents, "Never combine" or "Combine when full" can be easier because you see what is open.

Pinning programs (keep only what you use)

Pinned programs appear even when they are not running. They are your quick launch tools.

Safe approach:

Pin only what you use daily, like:

- Browser
- File Explorer (Windows Explorer)
- Word processor
- PDF reader

If you pin too many programs, it becomes noise.

To pin a program:

1. Click Start.
2. Find the program.
3. Right-click it.
4. Click **Pin to Taskbar**.

To unpin:

1. Right-click the icon.
2. Click **Unpin this program from taskbar**.

Notification area control (reducing clutter)

The notification area is where many programs place small icons. Too many icons mean too many background programs and too many distractions.

In Taskbar settings, look for:

- Notification area
- Customize

From there you can choose which icons appear.

Options include:

- Show icon and notifications
- Hide icon and notifications
- Only show notifications

Beginner safe approach:

- Keep only essential icons visible:

- Network
- Volume
- Battery (laptops)
- Security/antivirus (if installed)

Hide or limit other icons unless you truly need them.

Why this matters:

- Less clutter
- Fewer distractions
- Easier troubleshooting (you can spot real warnings faster)

Start menu settings (basic improvements)

The Start menu is your main launcher.

In Start Menu settings you can control:

- Which items appear
- Whether recently used programs appear
- Which folders show on the right side (Documents, Downloads, etc.)

Beginner friendly tips:

- Keep "Documents" and "Computer" visible.
- Use the Search box instead of digging through menus.

- Keep the Start menu simple.

If you find the Start menu crowded, remove items you do not use.

Display settings: readability and comfort

Display settings are not only about looks. They are about eye strain, productivity, and correct resolution.

Opening Display settings

1. Control Panel
2. Appearance and Personalization
3. Click **Display**

Here you can manage:

- Text size (DPI scaling)
- Resolution (often through "Screen resolution" link)
- ClearType text tuning (in some setups)

Text size: making Windows readable

Many beginners struggle because text is too small.

In Display settings, you may see options like:

- Smaller (default)
- Medium (125%)
- Larger (150%) (depends on setup)

Choosing a larger text size can make the computer much easier to use, especially on high-resolution screens.

Important:
When you change text size, Windows may require logoff/logon to apply changes.

Undo habit:

- Write down your original setting before changing.
- If the new setting looks strange, go back and restore.

Screen resolution basics

Resolution controls how many pixels are used to display content.

If resolution is wrong, you may see:

- Stretched screen
- Blurry text
- Icons too large or too small
- Black borders around the screen

Opening Screen Resolution

From Display settings, click **Screen resolution**.

You will see:

- Display selection (if multiple monitors)
- Resolution dropdown

- Orientation (landscape/portrait)
- Multiple displays settings (if supported)

The safe rule for resolution

Use the **Recommended** resolution.

Windows often labels it as "Recommended." That usually matches the monitor's native resolution.

If you choose a non-native resolution, things can look blurry.

What to do if you choose the wrong resolution

If you change resolution and the screen looks bad:

- Wait and click "Revert" when Windows asks.
- Or press Escape if you can't see properly.
- Windows usually reverts automatically if you do nothing.

Undo habit is built into resolution changes, but still record what you did.

ClearType (making text sharper)

Windows 7 includes ClearType to improve text clarity on LCD screens.

If text looks fuzzy:

- Search for "ClearType" in the Start menu and run "Adjust ClearType text."

- Follow the steps and choose the samples that look best to your eyes.

This is subjective. Choose what looks clear to you.

Fonts: useful, but be careful

Fonts control how text looks across programs. Windows 7 includes many fonts already, and most people never need to install more.

But installing fonts can carry risk when fonts come from unknown sources or are bundled with installers.

Opening Fonts

1. Control Panel
2. Appearance and Personalization
3. Click **Fonts**

Here you can:

- View installed fonts
- Preview fonts
- Install fonts by dragging them into the Fonts folder (or using install option)

When fonts are safe and useful

Fonts are useful if you:

- Do design work
- Write documents with specific typography needs

- Need a language font set

Safe sources are usually:

- Official vendors
- Reputable font libraries
- Fonts that come with trusted software

When to avoid installing fonts

Avoid installing fonts when:

- The font file comes from a random forum or unknown site
- The font is packaged inside an installer you do not trust
- The font download is bundled with toolbars or "download managers"

Fonts are not as risky as running unknown programs, but they are still files that can be abused in certain ways. On older systems, it is better to be cautious.

Safe habit:
If you do not truly need the font, do not install it.

"How to undo it" habit for fonts

If you install a font and later decide you should not have:

1. Open Fonts.
2. Find the font.

3. Delete it (or uninstall, depending on view).
4. Restart programs that were using it.

Before installing:

- Create a restore point if you are installing many fonts or using unknown sources.
- Write down what you installed.

Folder Options: the key safety habit

Folder Options is one of the most important settings areas in Windows 7.

It controls how folders behave and what you can see.

This is where you learn the habit that prevents file confusion and many malware tricks:

Show file extensions.

Why file extensions matter

A file extension is the part after the dot:

- .txt
- .doc
- .jpg
- .exe
- .pdf

Windows uses extensions to decide which program opens a file.

If file extensions are hidden, a dangerous file can disguise itself.

Example:

- A file named "Invoice.pdf.exe" might appear as "Invoice.pdf" if extensions are hidden.
- A beginner might double-click it thinking it is a PDF, but it is actually a program.

Showing extensions helps you see the truth.

Opening Folder Options

1. Control Panel
2. Appearance and Personalization
3. Click **Folder Options**

You will see tabs such as:

- General
- View
- Search

The most important tab for safety is:

- View

Turning on file extensions (do this first)

Steps:

1. Open Folder Options.

2. Click the **View** tab.
3. In Advanced settings, find:
   - "Hide extensions for known file types"
4. Uncheck it.
5. Click Apply.
6. Click OK.

Now file extensions will show.

This is one of the best beginner improvements you can make.

Undo habit:

- You can re-check it, but do not. Keep extensions visible.

Hidden files and folders (handle carefully)

Windows hides some files for safety.

In Folder Options, you will see options like:

- Don't show hidden files, folders, or drives
- Show hidden files, folders, and drives
- Hide protected operating system files (Recommended)

Beginner safe settings:

- Keep "Don't show hidden files" ON for normal daily use

- Keep "Hide protected operating system files" ON

Why?
Because hidden system files include important Windows files. Beginners can delete them accidentally.

When might you show hidden files?

- When troubleshooting specific issues and you know what you are looking for.

- When a trusted guide requires it.

If you do show hidden files:

- Return the setting back after troubleshooting.

That is the "how to undo it" habit.

Fixing "missing files" confusion using Folder Options

Many beginners say:

"My files disappeared."

In many cases, the files did not disappear. They are hidden, or you are looking in the wrong folder, or Windows is not showing file extensions.

Common causes of "missing files" confusion:

1. Files were saved in a different location
   Example: saved to Desktop in another user account.

2. Files are hidden
   Some malware hides files, or a user accidentally toggled hidden attributes.

3. File extensions are hidden and file names look unfamiliar
   Example: "Report" might actually be "Report.docx" and the user is searching wrong.

4. Viewing settings changed
   Example: Windows Explorer is not showing all files.

Folder Options helps you confirm what you are actually seeing.

A safe approach when someone thinks files are missing:

1. Confirm you are in the correct user account.

2. Check the folder path (Documents, Desktop, Downloads).

3. Search for the file name using Start menu search.

4. If still missing, check hidden file settings carefully.

5. Do not delete anything while investigating.

Practice tasks for Chapter 7

These tasks build comfort, clarity, and safer habits.

Practice Task 1: Turn on file extensions (must-do)

1. Open Folder Options.
2. View tab.
3. Uncheck "Hide extensions for known file types."
4. Apply and OK.

Test:

- Go to a folder with files and confirm you can see extensions like .txt, .jpg, .pdf.

Goal:
Remove confusion and reduce malware risk.

Practice Task 2: Clean taskbar layout

1. Right-click the taskbar and open Properties.
2. Choose a taskbar button setting that fits you:
    - Combine when full or Never combine (if you prefer clarity)
3. Click Customize in the notification area section.
4. Hide icons you do not need and keep only essentials visible.
5. Pin 3–5 programs you use daily and unpin the rest.

Goal:
A calmer, clearer workspace that improves daily use.

Practice Task 3: Adjust display for readability

1. Open Display settings.
2. Try Medium (125%) if text is too small.
3. Log off and log on if required.
4. Confirm it feels comfortable.

Undo:

- Return to default if it looks wrong.

Goal:
Reduce eye strain and make the PC easier to use.

Practice Task 4: Resolve a "missing file" confusion scenario

Create a small test:

1. Create a text file on the Desktop named "testfile.txt".
2. Confirm you see ".txt" at the end.
3. Move it into Documents.
4. Use Search to find it again.
5. Confirm that it did not disappear, it just moved.

Goal:
Build trust in your ability to find files calmly.

Chapter recap

- Appearance and Personalization affects comfort, productivity, and safety, not just looks.

- Personalization controls themes and desktop settings. Keep it simple and readable.

- Taskbar and Start Menu settings can reduce clutter and confusion. Control your notification area.

- Display settings improve readability and reduce eye strain. Use recommended resolution and sensible scaling.

- Fonts are useful, but avoid installing unknown font files or bundled installers.

- Folder Options is critical. Showing file extensions is a major safety improvement.

- Handle hidden files carefully and return settings back after troubleshooting.

- Practice tasks help you build habits: show extensions, clean taskbar, improve readability, and solve "missing file" confusion.

Next chapter preview

In Chapter 8, you will learn **Clock, Region, and Language**, including time zones, system clock accuracy, adding keyboard layouts, and setting correct formats for dates and numbers so Windows matches your real world.

CHAPTER 8: CLOCK, REGION, AND LANGUAGE

WHY THIS CHAPTER MATTERS

A wrong clock can break more things than most beginners expect.

When your Windows 7 date and time are incorrect, you may run into problems like these:

- Secure websites refuse to load, or show certificate warnings.

- Email timestamps look wrong, and messages appear out of order.

- File dates look confusing, and you cannot tell what is newest.

- Scheduled tasks run at the wrong time.

- Backups run at the wrong time, or do not run at all.

- Online logins fail because the computer time is too far off.

- Office or school systems reject your connection.

And even when the time is correct, the wrong "region" settings can cause daily frustration:

- Dates display as month/day/year when you expect day/month/year.

- Decimal points and commas are reversed, so numbers look wrong.

- Currency symbols do not match your location.

- Sorting and searching behave oddly for names and characters.

- You cannot type certain letters because the keyboard layout is wrong.

- You press one key and a different symbol appears.

This chapter helps you build a calm, reliable routine for time, formats, and typing. Once these settings are correct, many "mystery problems" disappear.

What lives in Clock, Region, and Language

In Control Panel (Category view), **Clock, Region, and Language** usually includes:

- **Date and Time**
- **Region and Language**

Inside these tools you can manage:

- Time zone
- Daylight Saving Time behavior (where applicable)
- Extra clocks for other time zones
- Date formats (short date, long date)
- Time formats (12-hour vs 24-hour)

- Number formats (decimal symbol, digit grouping)
- Currency formats
- Keyboard layouts
- Input languages

What kinds of problems this category solves

This category helps you solve problems like:

- "My computer time keeps changing."
- "The time is correct but the time zone is wrong."
- "My computer clock is slow or fast every week."
- "I work with another country and need a second clock."
- "My date shows 02/03/2026 and I cannot tell if it is February or March."
- "My Excel numbers behave strangely because commas and dots are mixed up."
- "I cannot type quotes, apostrophes, or certain letters correctly."
- "My keyboard suddenly started typing the wrong symbols."

Let's start with the most important tool here: Date and Time.

Date and Time

How to open Date and Time

Method 1 (Control Panel):

1. Open **Control Panel**
2. Click **Clock, Region, and Language**
3. Click **Date and Time**

Method 2 (taskbar clock):

1. Look at the clock in the bottom-right corner
2. Click the time/date
3. Click **Change date and time settings…**

Both lead to the same place.

Understanding the Date and Time window

In Windows 7, the Date and Time settings window usually has tabs like:

- **Date and Time**
- **Additional Clocks**
- **Internet Time** (on many systems)

The three most important skills are:

1. Set the correct **time zone**
2. Set the correct **date and time**
3. Keep the clock accurate over time (reduce drift)

Time zone basics

A time zone is not the same thing as the time.

Two computers can show different local times while both are correct, because they are in different time zones.

A common beginner mistake is fixing the clock by changing the time manually, but leaving the time zone wrong. That can cause confusion later, especially when Daylight Saving Time changes (in places that use it), or when you travel.

How to set the correct time zone

1. Open **Date and Time**
2. Click **Change time zone…**
3. Select the correct time zone from the list
4. Click OK

If your region uses Daylight Saving Time, you will see a checkbox like:

- "Automatically adjust clock for Daylight Saving Time"

If your region does not use it, you may not need that setting, and in some cases the option is not present depending on the time zone chosen.

Safe habit:

- Set the correct time zone first.
- Then correct the time.

Signs your time zone is wrong

- The clock is off by exactly 1 hour, 2 hours, 6 hours, and so on.
- The clock changes when you restart, but always returns to the wrong offset.
- Calendar appointments look shifted.
- A travel laptop shows the previous country's time.

If the clock is off by a consistent number of hours, time zone is the first thing to check.

Setting the date and time

After time zone is correct, set the time:

1. Open **Date and Time**
2. Click **Change date and time…**
3. Adjust the calendar for the correct date
4. Adjust the time
5. Click OK

Safe habit:

- Do not rush.
- Confirm AM vs PM if you use 12-hour time.
- Confirm the year, especially on older PCs after battery issues.

Why a wrong clock causes website and login problems

Secure websites use certificates with valid date ranges. If your computer time is wrong, Windows may think a valid certificate is "not yet valid" or "expired."

That is why you might see warnings like:

- Certificate error
- Secure connection failed
- Your connection is not private (wording varies by browser)

Many beginners think this means the website is hacked. Sometimes it is simply the computer clock.

If a website suddenly fails, check your time and date before changing browsers or security settings.

What causes clock drift

Clock drift means the computer time slowly becomes inaccurate.

Windows 7 systems can drift for several reasons:

1) Weak or dead CMOS battery

Most desktop motherboards and many laptops have a small battery that keeps time when the computer is off. When it becomes weak:

- The clock resets when the PC is unplugged.

- The date may jump backward, sometimes to a much older year.

- BIOS settings can reset.

Common signs:

- Every time you turn the PC on after it was unplugged, the time is wrong again.

- The date resets to a default value.

- You see a message at startup about BIOS settings or time.

Fix:

- Replace the CMOS battery (usually a CR2032 coin battery on many desktops). This is a hardware task, so if you are not comfortable opening a PC, ask a technician.

2) No time synchronization

If your system does not sync time, small drift can build up.

Windows can sync with an internet time server (when enabled and allowed by network policy).

3) Sleep, hibernate, and older hardware quirks

Some older systems drift more noticeably after long sleep or hibernate cycles, especially if drivers or BIOS firmware are old. This is less common than battery issues, but it happens.

4) Dual-boot systems and time conflicts

If a computer runs another operating system alongside Windows, time handling can conflict, depending on how each system stores time. This is more advanced, but it can cause repeated shifts.

5) Malware or misconfigured software

Less common, but possible:

- Some malicious or broken software changes time settings.

- Some "optimizer" tools meddle with system settings.

Safe habit:
If your time keeps changing unexpectedly, consider scanning the system with trusted security tools and reviewing recently installed programs.

Internet Time (time synchronization)

Many Windows 7 systems include an **Internet Time** tab.

This allows Windows to periodically sync its time with a time server.

How to enable or check Internet time sync

1. Open **Date and Time**

2. Click the **Internet Time** tab

3. Click **Change settings…**

4. Check "Synchronize with an Internet time server"

5. Choose a server (Windows usually provides a default)
6. Click **Update now**
7. Click OK

If the update succeeds, your time is now aligned.

If it fails, possible reasons include:

- No internet access
- Firewall or network policy blocking time sync
- Company network rules
- Incorrect proxy settings

Beginner safe troubleshooting:

- Confirm internet works.
- Confirm time zone is correct.
- Try Update now again.
- If this is a work PC, ask IT if time sync is managed centrally.

"How to undo it" habit for Date and Time changes

Time settings affect many parts of the computer. Whenever you change time settings, write a simple note:

- Date: (today)

- Change made: time zone changed from X to Y, time corrected, sync enabled or disabled
- Result: websites now load, email timestamps fixed, scheduling fixed

If a change creates confusion, you can return and restore the previous setting quickly.

Adding extra clocks for other time zones

Why extra clocks help

Extra clocks are useful when:

- You work with a team in another country.
- You coordinate calls across time zones.
- You manage clients or family in another region.
- You travel often and want a reference clock.

Windows 7 lets you add extra clocks that appear when you hover over the taskbar clock.

This is a simple feature, but it reduces mental math and scheduling mistakes.

How to add extra clocks

1. Open **Date and Time**
2. Click the **Additional Clocks** tab
3. Check "Show this clock" for Clock 1

4. Select a time zone for Clock 1

5. Enter a display name (example: "London" or "Nairobi" or "Home")

6. Check "Show this clock" for Clock 2 (optional)

7. Choose its time zone and name

8. Click OK

Now, when you hover over the clock, you will see multiple times.

Naming your clocks clearly

Use names that match your real use:

- "Home"
- "Office"
- "Client"
- "Family"
- "UTC"

Avoid confusing labels like "Clock 1."

Common mistakes with extra clocks

- Setting the extra clock to the same time zone as the main clock, by accident.
- Naming the clock incorrectly and forgetting what it represents.

- Using extra clocks as a substitute for fixing the main time zone.

Safe rule:

- Fix main time zone first.
- Then add extra clocks.

Region and Language

Time and date are only one part of how Windows matches your real world. The other major part is formatting and input.

What Region and Language controls

Region and Language controls:

- Date format (short and long)
- Time format (12-hour or 24-hour)
- Number format (decimal symbol, thousands separator)
- Currency format (symbol, decimals)
- Measurement units (depending on settings)
- Keyboard layouts and input languages
- Location (in some setups)

If you ever see numbers that look wrong, or dates that confuse you, this is the place to fix it.

How to open Region and Language

1. Open **Control Panel**

2. Click **Clock, Region, and Language**

3. Click **Region and Language**

You will usually see tabs such as:

- **Formats**
- **Location** (may vary)
- **Keyboards and Languages**
- **Administrative** (advanced)

Beginners mainly use Formats and Keyboards and Languages.

Formats: date, time, and number formats

Choosing the correct format for your region

In the Formats tab, you can choose a format from a dropdown list.

This setting affects how Windows displays:

- Dates in file explorer
- Dates in many programs
- Time style
- Currency style
- Number separators

If your format is wrong, you may see:

- Dates that are hard to interpret
- Numbers that look incorrect

- Currency with the wrong symbol

Safe habit:
Choose the format that matches how you actually write dates and numbers daily.

Short date vs long date

Windows uses two main date displays:

Short date examples:

- 02/03/2026
- 03/02/2026
- 2026-02-03

Long date examples:

- Tuesday, February 3, 2026
- Tuesday, 3 February 2026

Short date can be confusing because 02/03 can mean February 3 or March 2 depending on the region.

If you regularly work with people across regions, consider a short date format that reduces confusion, such as:

- 2026-02-03 (year-month-day)

You can often customize this in "Additional settings," depending on Windows 7 options.

Time format: 12-hour vs 24-hour

Some people prefer:

- 12-hour time (with AM/PM)
  Others prefer:
- 24-hour time

Neither is "more correct." The best choice is what reduces errors for you.

If you work with schedules and travel, 24-hour time can reduce AM/PM mistakes.

Number formats and why they matter

Numbers can be displayed differently across regions.

Examples:

- Decimal symbol: dot or comma
- Thousands separator: comma, dot, or space

If the computer uses a comma as decimal separator, you might see:

- 1,50 meaning one and a half

If it uses a dot as decimal separator, you might see:

- 1.50 meaning one and a half

This matters in spreadsheets and accounting.

A common beginner issue:

- Copying a number from a website into a spreadsheet, then it is treated as text or becomes a different value.

If you work with finance or spreadsheets, confirm your number format matches your daily use.

Changing formats safely

1. Open Region and Language
2. Formats tab
3. Choose a format from the dropdown
4. Click Apply
5. Check a date display in the taskbar and in a folder
6. Check a number display in a spreadsheet if you use one

Undo habit:

- If it looks wrong, return and pick the previous format.

Keyboards and Languages: typing the right characters

Why keyboard layout matters

Your physical keyboard has keys, but Windows decides what each key means through the keyboard layout.

That is why two people can press the same key and get different symbols, because their layout is different.

Common beginner problem:

- You press a key expecting "@" but something else appears.
- You press a key expecting a quote, but it types a different symbol.
- Letters appear scrambled because layout changed.

Input language vs keyboard layout

In simple terms:

- Input language affects spelling tools and language behavior.
- Keyboard layout affects what characters keys produce.

You might use English input language but add a different keyboard layout.

How to add a keyboard layout or input language

1. Open **Region and Language**
2. Click the **Keyboards and Languages** tab
3. Click **Change keyboards...**
4. In the General tab, click **Add...**
5. Choose the language
6. Expand it and select the keyboard layout you want
7. Click OK

8. Click Apply

Now you can switch between layouts.

How to switch between keyboard layouts

Windows 7 often shows a language indicator near the taskbar clock, such as:

- EN
- FR
- AR

You can click it to switch.

There are also keyboard shortcuts that may switch layouts (varies by setup). If your keyboard suddenly types differently, you may have triggered a layout switch shortcut.

Safe habit:

- Keep only the layouts you actually use.
- Too many layouts make accidental switching more likely.

Setting the default keyboard

In the "Text Services and Input Languages" window (the Change keyboards area), you can choose a default input language.

Set the one you use most as default.

This reduces surprises at login and after restart.

Removing an unwanted keyboard layout

If you have layouts you do not need:

1. Region and Language
2. Keyboards and Languages
3. Change keyboards
4. Select the unwanted layout
5. Click Remove
6. Apply

This is one of the best fixes for "my keyboard is typing wrong" when the issue is accidental switching.

Administrative tab (beginner awareness)

The Administrative tab includes system-wide language settings and options that affect non-Unicode programs and welcome screen behavior.

Beginner safe advice:

- Do not change Administrative settings unless you have a clear reason.
- If you do, write down the original values first.

These changes can affect how older programs display characters and how system accounts behave.

Troubleshooting: common time and language issues

Problem 1: The clock is wrong by exactly a few hours

Likely cause:

- Wrong time zone

Fix:

- Change time zone to correct one
- Confirm Daylight Saving Time setting (if applicable)

Problem 2: The clock resets when the computer is off

Likely cause:

- Weak CMOS battery

Fix:

- Replace battery (hardware task)
- Then set correct time zone and time again

Problem 3: Secure websites show certificate warnings

Likely cause:

- Wrong system date/time

Fix:

- Correct date and time
- Enable time sync if possible

- Restart browser and try again

Problem 4: Dates are confusing and you cannot tell day vs month

Likely cause:

- Wrong regional format

Fix:

- Change Formats setting
- Consider using a less ambiguous short date format if available

Problem 5: Numbers in spreadsheets act strange

Likely cause:

- Decimal symbol and separators do not match your expectation

Fix:

- Check Region and Language number format
- Confirm how your spreadsheet expects decimals

Problem 6: Keyboard types wrong symbols

Likely cause:

- Wrong keyboard layout selected, or accidental switching

Fix:

- Check language indicator in taskbar
- Switch back to correct layout
- Remove unwanted layouts to prevent future confusion

Practice tasks for Chapter 8

These practice tasks build real skill. Do them carefully, and write down what you change.

Practice Task 1: Set the correct time zone

1. Open Date and Time.
2. Click Change time zone.
3. Choose your correct time zone.
4. Click OK.
5. Confirm the time now makes sense.

Quick check:

- Compare with your phone time (phones usually sync automatically).

Undo habit:

- If you chose the wrong one, return and correct it immediately.

Practice Task 2: Correct the system time and confirm stability

1. Open Date and Time.
2. Click Change date and time.

3. Set correct date and time.
4. Click OK.
5. Restart the computer.
6. Confirm the time stayed correct after restart.

If the time changes again after power off:

- Suspect battery issues.

Practice Task 3: Add an extra clock for another time zone

1. Open Date and Time.
2. Additional Clocks tab.
3. Enable Clock 1.
4. Choose a time zone you often work with.
5. Name it clearly (example: "Office").
6. Click OK.
7. Hover over the taskbar clock and confirm both clocks show.

Goal:
Reduce scheduling mistakes without mental math.

Practice Task 4: Confirm date and number formats are correct

1. Open Region and Language.
2. Formats tab.

3. Confirm:
   - Short date format matches your daily writing style
   - Time format matches your preference
   - Number format looks normal for you (decimal symbol, digit grouping)
4. Click Apply if you change anything.
5. Open a folder and confirm dates display as expected.
6. If you use spreadsheets, open one and type a simple number like 1.5 or 1,5 and confirm it behaves as expected.

Undo habit:

- If anything looks wrong, return and restore your previous format.

Practice Task 5: Add a keyboard layout and test it

1. Open Region and Language.
2. Keyboards and Languages tab.
3. Change keyboards.
4. Add a second keyboard layout you actually need.
5. Apply.

6. Use the language indicator to switch layouts.

7. Type a short test sentence in each layout.

Safety tip:

- If you do not need the layout daily, remove it after practice to avoid accidental switching.

Practice Task 6: Reduce accidental layout switching

1. Review the list of installed input languages.

2. Remove any you do not use.

3. Set your main layout as default.

Goal:
Stop surprise symbol changes while typing.

Chapter recap

- Date and Time settings affect security, browsing, email, backups, and scheduling.

- Always set the correct time zone first, then correct time and date.

- Clock drift is often caused by a weak CMOS battery or lack of time sync.

- Extra clocks are a simple, powerful tool for cross-time-zone work.

- Region and Language controls how dates, numbers, and currency appear.

- Keyboard layouts decide what keys type. Keep only what you use to avoid confusion.

- Practice tasks build habits: correct time zone, add an extra clock, confirm formats, and manage keyboard layouts.

Next chapter preview

In Chapter 9, you will learn **Ease of Access**, including built-in tools that make Windows 7 easier to read, easier to hear, and easier to control. You will also learn safe accessibility shortcuts that help in emergencies, like when the screen becomes hard to read or the mouse stops responding.

CHAPTER 9: EASE OF ACCESS

WHY THIS CHAPTER MATTERS

Most beginners think Ease of Access is only for people with disabilities. That is not true. In Windows 7, Ease of Access tools are helpful for everyone in real, everyday moments:

- The text is too small and you need to read something fast.

- The mouse stops responding and you need keyboard control.

- The screen looks strange and you need high contrast.

- A family member has hearing or vision challenges and needs the computer to be comfortable.

- You are tired, your eyes hurt, and you want the screen to be gentler.

- You accidentally triggered StickyKeys and now the keyboard is acting weird.

Ease of Access is also a troubleshooting friend. It gives you emergency tools to keep working when something goes wrong.

The key to using these features is this:

Use them on purpose, and know how to turn them off cleanly.

That "turn it on and back off cleanly" habit is what separates confident users from frustrated users.

What lives in Ease of Access

In Control Panel (Category view), **Ease of Access** usually includes:

- **Ease of Access Center**
- Links to set up or change accessibility options, including:
    - Display and vision aids
    - Hearing support
    - Keyboard and mouse options
    - Speech Recognition

Most tools can be reached from:

Ease of Access Center

That is your main dashboard for accessibility settings.

What kinds of problems this category solves

Ease of Access helps with:

- Reading small text quickly
- Improving contrast and visibility
- Using visual notifications when sound is not enough
- Preventing repeated keystrokes when hands are shaky or tired
- Using the keyboard instead of the mouse

- Using the mouse through the keyboard when the mouse is broken

- Controlling the PC by voice (basic Speech Recognition)

- Fixing accidental StickyKeys activation and other "keyboard gone strange" issues

Let's start with the hub: Ease of Access Center.

Ease of Access Center overview

How to open Ease of Access Center

Method 1 (Control Panel):

1. Open Control Panel.
2. Click **Ease of Access**.
3. Click **Ease of Access Center**.

Method 2 (keyboard shortcut):

- Press **Windows key + U**

This is worth remembering. If your mouse is not working, Windows key + U can open accessibility options quickly.

What you see inside

Ease of Access Center typically shows:

- Quick access links to common tools (Magnifier, Narrator, On-Screen Keyboard)

- Options to make the computer easier to use:
    - Make the computer easier to see
    - Make the computer easier to hear
    - Make the keyboard easier to use
    - Make the mouse easier to use
    - Use text or visual alternatives for sounds
    - Speech Recognition (depending on system)

It also often includes a short questionnaire or recommendations:

- "Get recommendations to make your computer easier to use"

Beginners can ignore the questionnaire at first and focus on learning the tools.

Vision aids: Magnifier, Narrator, High Contrast

These features help people with vision difficulty, but they also help any user in specific situations.

Magnifier

What Magnifier does

Magnifier zooms in on part of the screen. This helps when:

- Text is too small on a website.

- You need to read tiny numbers in a dialog box.

- You need to see fine detail in an image or map.

- You are presenting and want to highlight something.

How to turn Magnifier on

From Ease of Access Center:

1. Click **Start Magnifier**.

Or use the Windows shortcut:

- Windows key + (plus) to zoom in

- Windows key + (minus) to zoom out

(Exact behavior can vary, but Windows 7 supports keyboard zoom controls.)

Magnifier modes

Magnifier in Windows 7 typically offers modes such as:

- Full-screen mode (entire screen is zoomed)

- Lens mode (a lens follows your pointer)

- Docked mode (a zoomed strip appears at the top)

Beginner-friendly mode:

- Lens mode is often easiest for quick reading.

How to turn Magnifier off cleanly

This is important.

- Close the Magnifier window using the X button, or
- In Magnifier, choose Exit, or
- Use the keyboard to focus the Magnifier window and close it.

If you forget and leave it running, you may think the computer is "stuck zoomed." It is not broken. Magnifier is still on.

Undo habit:

- Always turn it off when you finish using it.

Narrator

What Narrator does

Narrator is a screen reader. It reads text and UI elements aloud.

Narrator helps:

- People with limited vision
- Users who want audio feedback while learning menus
- Anyone testing accessibility

In Windows 7, Narrator is basic compared to dedicated screen readers, but it can still help in simple tasks.

How to start Narrator

From Ease of Access Center:

1. Click **Start Narrator**.

Narrator will begin reading elements as you move around.

How to stop Narrator

Narrator can feel "too loud" if you started it by accident.

To stop it:

- Close the Narrator window
- Or return to Ease of Access Center and turn it off
- If needed, use Task Manager as a last resort (advanced step)

Safe habit:

- Start Narrator only when you intend to use it.

High Contrast

What High Contrast does

High Contrast changes the color scheme so text and elements stand out strongly. It helps when:

- You have eye strain
- You are in bright sunlight

- The screen is hard to read
- You want clear separation between text and background

High Contrast can be a major improvement for comfort.

How to enable High Contrast

You can enable it through:

- Ease of Access Center, or
- Personalization settings, or
- Shortcut keys (depending on system)

The exact shortcut can vary, and some systems prompt before enabling.

Beginner safe advice:
Enable it from Ease of Access Center so you can easily reverse it.

How to turn High Contrast off

Return to the same place and disable it, or choose a normal theme again.

Undo habit:

- If someone says "my screen looks weird," one of the first checks is whether High Contrast was turned on accidentally.

Hearing support: captions and visual alerts

Windows 7 includes options for people with hearing difficulty, but these features can also help in noisy environments or quiet offices.

Visual alternatives for sounds

Windows can show visual cues when sounds occur, such as:

- Flashing the screen or active window
- Showing captions for some system events

This is useful when:

- The sound is muted
- Speakers are broken
- You are in a meeting and sound is off

Where to find these settings

In Ease of Access Center, look for options like:

- "Use text or visual alternatives for sounds"
- "Turn on visual notifications for sounds"

You may see choices like:

- Flash the title bar
- Flash the active window
- Flash the entire screen

Beginner safe option:

- Flash the title bar or active window, not the entire screen, unless you truly need strong alerts.

Captions

Windows 7 includes caption-related options, but it does not automatically caption all audio. Captions are more useful in media players or websites that support them.

However, Ease of Access includes options like:

- Make captioning easier to read
- Adjust caption appearance (where supported)

Beginner advice:

- Use captions where the app or website supports it.
- Use Ease of Access caption settings to improve readability if you rely on captions.

Mobility support: StickyKeys, FilterKeys, Mouse Keys

These features are very useful, but they are also the source of many beginner panic moments because they can be turned on accidentally.

If you learn them now, you will not fear them later.

StickyKeys

What StickyKeys does

StickyKeys lets you press modifier keys one at a time instead of holding them down.

Modifier keys include:

- Shift
- Ctrl
- Alt
- Windows key

This helps people who have difficulty holding two keys at once.

Example:
Instead of holding Ctrl and pressing C, you can press Ctrl, release, then press C.

The most common beginner problem: StickyKeys turns on accidentally

StickyKeys can be triggered by pressing Shift five times in a row.

Many people do this by accident when:

- They are gaming
- They are typing fast
- They are frustrated and tapping keys

When StickyKeys turns on, the keyboard feels "weird" because modifier keys behave differently.

How to fix accidental StickyKeys activation

If you see a StickyKeys prompt or notice weird behavior:

1. Look for the StickyKeys dialog that appears.
2. Choose to turn StickyKeys off.
3. If it keeps returning, go into Ease of Access Center:
    - Make the keyboard easier to use
    - Find StickyKeys settings
    - Turn it off and disable the shortcut if needed

Safe habit:
If you never need StickyKeys, disable the shortcut that turns it on with Shift five times.

Turning StickyKeys off and preventing surprise activation

Steps:

1. Open Ease of Access Center (Windows key + U is fastest).
2. Click "Make the keyboard easier to use."
3. Find StickyKeys.
4. Uncheck "Turn on StickyKeys."
5. Click "Set up StickyKeys" (or similar link).
6. Disable the shortcut option:

- "Turn on StickyKeys when SHIFT is pressed five times"

7. Apply and OK.

Undo habit:

- If a user needs StickyKeys later, you can turn it back on knowingly.

FilterKeys

What FilterKeys does

FilterKeys helps by ignoring brief or repeated keystrokes. It is useful when:

- Hands shake
- Keys are pressed accidentally
- A keyboard repeats letters too easily

But it can confuse beginners because it can make the keyboard feel "slow" or unresponsive.

FilterKeys can also be triggered accidentally, depending on shortcut settings.

If typing feels delayed, check FilterKeys.

Turning FilterKeys off

In Ease of Access Center:

1. Make the keyboard easier to use
2. Find FilterKeys
3. Turn it off

4. Consider disabling the shortcut that activates it

Mouse Keys

What Mouse Keys does

Mouse Keys lets you move the mouse pointer using the keyboard, usually the numeric keypad.

This helps when:

- The mouse is broken
- You cannot use a mouse comfortably
- You need temporary control

It can also confuse users if turned on by accident because the keypad starts moving the pointer instead of typing numbers.

How to turn Mouse Keys on

In Ease of Access Center:

- Make the mouse easier to use
- Turn on Mouse Keys

How to turn Mouse Keys off

Return to the same setting and disable it.

Undo habit:

- If your numeric keypad behaves strangely, Mouse Keys is one of the first checks.

Speech Recognition basics

Speech Recognition lets you control the computer and dictate text with your voice.

In Windows 7, Speech Recognition works best when:

- You have a decent microphone
- You speak clearly
- You train it a little
- You use it in a quieter environment

It is not magic. It is a tool that improves with practice.

What Speech Recognition can do (basic)

Speech Recognition can:

- Open programs (some commands)
- Click menus and buttons by voice (with practice)
- Dictate text into supported programs
- Perform basic navigation

It may not work equally well in all programs, and it may require patience.

Setting up Speech Recognition

Speech Recognition setup typically includes:

1. Choosing a microphone
2. Running a microphone setup wizard

3. Doing a short training session
4. Turning on recognition and testing commands

To begin:

1. Open Control Panel.
2. Ease of Access.
3. Look for Speech Recognition options.
4. Start the setup wizard.

If you do not see it, your Windows edition or installed features may differ, but most Windows 7 systems include it.

Microphone setup matters

Most recognition failures are microphone failures, not speech failures.

Beginner tips:

- Use a headset microphone if possible.
- Keep the microphone close to your mouth but not touching.
- Avoid loud fans or background noise.
- Speak naturally, not like a robot, but clearly.

Simple training tips

Speech Recognition improves when you train it.

Beginner training habits:

1. Do the built-in training session once
2. Dictate short sentences daily for a week
3. Correct mistakes using the correction tools
4. Use a consistent microphone and environment

Do not expect perfect accuracy immediately. Treat it like learning a new input skill.

When Speech Recognition is not the best option

Speech Recognition may not be ideal when:

- The environment is very noisy
- You share a room and privacy matters
- The microphone quality is poor
- You need very precise technical text with many symbols

In those cases, using keyboard and mouse is often faster.

Practice tasks for Chapter 9

This chapter's practice is about control: turning features on deliberately, and turning them off cleanly.

Practice Task 1: Use Magnifier for 2 minutes, then exit cleanly

1. Open Ease of Access Center.
2. Start Magnifier.
3. Zoom in and read a small piece of text.
4. Change the mode (try Lens or Docked if available).
5. Exit Magnifier cleanly.

Goal:
Learn that Magnifier is a tool, not a problem.

Practice Task 2: Turn on High Contrast, then restore normal display

1. Open Ease of Access Center.
2. Enable High Contrast.
3. Observe the change.
4. Turn it off and return to your normal theme.

Goal:
Know how to fix "my screen looks weird" quickly.

Practice Task 3: Trigger StickyKeys accidentally on purpose, then fix it

This sounds funny, but it teaches confidence.

1. Press Shift five times quickly.
2. When the StickyKeys prompt appears, turn it on briefly.
3. Type a few keys and notice behavior.

4. Turn StickyKeys off.

5. Go into StickyKeys settings and disable the shortcut so it does not surprise you later.

Goal:
Stop fearing StickyKeys and learn prevention.

Practice Task 4: Explore Mouse Keys, then turn it off

1. Open Ease of Access Center.

2. Turn on Mouse Keys.

3. Move the pointer using the numeric keypad for a moment.

4. Turn it off.

Goal:
Have a backup method if your mouse fails.

Practice Task 5: Start Speech Recognition setup (optional)

If you have a microphone:

1. Open Speech Recognition.

2. Run microphone setup.

3. Run one training session.

4. Dictate a short paragraph into a text editor.

5. Turn Speech Recognition off.

Goal:
Understand the basics and learn the on/off control habit.

Quick troubleshooting section

Problem: "My keyboard is typing weird and shortcut keys are stuck"

Most likely cause:

- StickyKeys is on

Fix:

- Turn off StickyKeys in Ease of Access Center
- Disable the Shift five times shortcut if not needed

Problem: "My keyboard feels slow and letters don't repeat normally"

Most likely cause:

- FilterKeys is on

Fix:

- Turn off FilterKeys in keyboard Ease of Access settings

Problem: "My numeric keypad moves the mouse instead of typing numbers"

Most likely cause:

- Mouse Keys is on

Fix:

- Turn off Mouse Keys

Problem: "My screen suddenly looks high-contrast or strange"

Most likely cause:

- High Contrast mode was enabled

Fix:

- Turn it off and restore normal theme

Chapter recap

- Ease of Access tools help everyone, not only people with disabilities.

- Ease of Access Center is the hub, and Windows key + U opens it quickly.

- Vision aids: Magnifier for zoom, Narrator for basic reading aloud, High Contrast for strong visibility.

- Hearing support: visual alerts and caption settings help in quiet or noisy environments.

- Mobility support: StickyKeys, FilterKeys, and Mouse Keys can help but often confuse when enabled accidentally.

- Speech Recognition can be useful with a good microphone and a little training.

- The key skill is turning features on intentionally and turning them off cleanly, plus disabling accidental shortcuts when needed.

Next chapter preview

In Chapter 10, you will learn **Windows Update and Maintenance routines**, including simple weekly checks, reading update history, and building a calm "maintenance habit" that keeps a Windows 7 computer stable without constant tinkering.

CHAPTER 10: WRAP-UP AND NEXT STEPS

WHAT YOU SHOULD NOW BE ABLE TO DO WITH CONFIDENCE

If you have worked through this book chapter by chapter, you have done something many Windows 7 users never do. You did not just "use a computer." You learned how Windows 7 is organized, why settings exist, and how to make changes safely without turning the system into a guessing game.

At this point, you should be able to do the following with calm confidence.

You can navigate the Control Panel without fear

You know that Control Panel is not one big mystery room. It is a set of organized categories that each solve a specific kind of problem. When something breaks, you can usually guess which category is relevant:

- Security or system issues lead you toward System and Security.

- Network problems lead you toward Network and Internet.

- Printers and audio lead you toward Hardware and Sound.

- File confusion and desktop habits lead you toward Appearance and Personalization.

- Time and typing issues lead you toward Clock, Region, and Language.

- Accessibility and "keyboard acting strange" problems lead you toward Ease of Access.

- Software removal and defaults lead you toward Programs.

- Shared PC issues lead you toward User Accounts and Family Safety.

That mental map is a serious skill. It saves time, reduces stress, and prevents random clicking.

You can open key tools in multiple ways

Beginners often rely on one path and feel lost if the menu looks different. You now know multiple ways to open the same tool, which is exactly how IT support works in real life.

Examples you should now be comfortable with:

- Opening Control Panel from Start.

- Finding settings using Start menu search.

- Opening Ease of Access Center with Windows key + U.

- Opening Date and Time by clicking the taskbar clock.

- Getting to taskbar settings by right-clicking the taskbar.

- Getting to personalization by right-clicking the desktop.

This makes you resilient. Even if the PC is configured differently, you can still find what you need.

You can change settings safely, with a plan to undo

This may be the most important skill you learned.

You now understand that "clicking around" is not troubleshooting. Troubleshooting is controlled testing.

You practiced a habit that keeps you safe:

1. Change one thing at a time
2. Test immediately
3. Write down what you changed
4. Know how to reverse it

That habit will protect you from your own mistakes and from "helpful" advice online that breaks machines.

You can solve common daily problems

You should now be able to handle these problems without needing a technician for the first step:

- A computer that says "no internet"
- A printer that will not print
- A system that has "no sound"
- A file type opening in the wrong program

- A desktop that is cluttered and confusing

- A taskbar that is noisy and distracting

- A computer clock that is wrong and breaks secure websites

- A keyboard that types the wrong symbols because the layout changed

- A screen that suddenly looks strange because High Contrast or Magnifier is on

- StickyKeys activating and making the keyboard behave oddly

You may not solve every case perfectly, but you now know where to start and how to avoid causing damage while you test.

You understand the security basics that keep beginners safe

Windows 7 is an older system, and that means you must be extra careful. But even on newer systems, the principles remain the same.

You have learned security habits that reduce risk:

- Using Standard accounts for daily work instead of Admin accounts.

- Treating UAC prompts as meaningful warnings, not as noise.

- Being careful with AutoPlay.

- Avoiding unknown fonts, gadgets, and bundled installers.

- Showing file extensions so you can see what a file truly is.

- Keeping sharing off on public networks.

These habits are more valuable than any single "antivirus tip," because they reduce the chance of trouble in the first place.

A simple maintenance routine that actually works

Many people ruin their computers by doing too much "maintenance." They install random cleaners, they delete things they do not understand, they disable services, or they run optimization tools that cause more problems than they solve.

Good maintenance is simple and consistent. Think of it like brushing your teeth. You do not do surgery every day. You do small actions that prevent big problems.

Here is a practical maintenance routine you can follow.

Daily or every time you use the computer (2 minutes)

1. Notice warning signs
   Before you start work, glance at the basics:

- Is the time and date correct?

- Is the network icon normal (connected if you expect it)?

- Are there unusual pop-ups or repeated prompts?

If something looks wrong, pause and investigate before you continue.

2. Save your work properly
Do not rely on "it will auto-save." Make saving a habit, especially on older systems.

3. Avoid risky behavior

- Do not install random programs "to try them."

- Do not click unknown attachments.

- Do not plug unknown USB drives into your main PC.

Daily safety is mostly about what you do not do.

Weekly routine (15 to 30 minutes)

A weekly routine is enough for most home users.

Step 1: Check Windows Update status

Even though Windows 7 is older, you may still be in an environment where updates are managed locally or via company policy. Some systems have updates disabled, others use internal update servers, and some rely on manual patching practices.

Your goal each week is not to change update policies blindly. Your goal is to check status and confirm nothing is obviously wrong.

What to do:

- Open Control Panel.
- Go to System and Security.
- Open Windows Update (if available on your system).
- Check whether updates are enabled.
- Check if there are failed updates or repeated errors.
- Review update history for patterns.

If you see repeated failures:

- Write down the error code.
- Try basic steps like restart.
- If you are on a managed/work PC, report it to IT.

If you are at home and you do not understand update settings:

- Do not change them in panic.
- At minimum, record what the settings are so you can ask someone knowledgeable.

Step 2: Do a quick storage check

Low disk space causes slow performance and weird behavior.

Once a week:

- Open Computer.
- Check free space on the system drive (usually C:).

A simple rule of thumb for beginners:
Keep several gigabytes free, and ideally keep at least 10 to 20 percent of the drive free if possible.

If space is low:

- Uninstall programs you truly do not use (using Programs and Features).
- Move large personal files (videos, photos) to an external drive.
- Empty the Recycle Bin after verifying what is inside.

Avoid:

- Deleting system folders.
- Deleting random files you do not recognize.
- Using aggressive "registry cleaners."

Step 3: Backup your important files

Backups are not optional if you care about your work.

A beginner-friendly backup approach:

- Identify what matters:
    - Documents

- Photos
- Writing projects
- Spreadsheets
- Important downloads

- Choose a backup location:
  - External hard drive
  - USB drive (for smaller sets)
  - A trusted cloud option (if you have stable internet)

- Make a weekly copy routine:
  - Copy the key folders
  - Confirm the files actually copied
  - Keep at least one backup separate from the computer

Many people believe they "have backups" because files exist somewhere. A real backup is one you can restore from.

So each week, test one small restore:

- Copy one file back from the backup location into a test folder and open it.

That proves your backup is real.

Step 4: Quick health check

A simple weekly health check can include:

- Restart the computer (a clean restart clears many minor issues).

- Confirm sound works (play a short audio clip).

- Confirm internet works (open one trusted site).

- Confirm printing works (only if you print often).

The goal is not to test every feature. The goal is to catch issues early before you need the computer urgently.

Monthly routine (30 to 60 minutes)

Once a month, do slightly deeper checks.

Step 1: Review installed programs

- Open Programs and Features.
- Sort by Installed On.
- Look for programs you do not recognize.

If you see something suspicious:

- Do not uninstall blindly if you are not sure.
- Search the name online using a trusted source, or ask someone experienced.
- If it is clearly unwanted, uninstall it.

This simple review helps you catch toolbars and junk early.

Step 2: Review browser add-ons and startup clutter

This is not always in Control Panel, but it is related to program health.

If the computer feels slow at startup:

- Too many programs may be loading.

As a beginner, your safe move is to:

- Uninstall what you do not need.
- Avoid "startup manager" tools unless you understand them.

Step 3: Confirm account safety

Once a month, check:

- Who has admin rights?
- Are there accounts that should be removed or disabled?
- Are passwords still known by the rightful owners?

If a child account accidentally became admin, fix it.

If the same password is shared by everyone, consider separating accounts properly.

Quick health checks: a simple "three questions" method

When something feels wrong, don't jump into big fixes. Ask three questions first:

1. Is the issue only in one program, or everywhere?

- If only one program, fix the program.
- If everywhere, check system settings.

2. Did anything change recently?

- New software
- New updates
- New devices
- New network
- New account changes

3. Can I undo the last change I made?

- If yes, undo and test.
- If no, stop making new changes and start documenting.

This method prevents you from stacking mistakes.

Safe next learning steps for readers moving toward IT support or junior admin work

If you want to go beyond personal use and move toward helping others, you can start building professional habits. You do not need to become an expert overnight. You need to become reliable.

Here are safe, practical learning steps that build real capability.

1) Learn how to take good problem reports

When someone says "it's not working," you need details.

Practice asking:

- What exactly is not working?
- When did it last work?
- What changed before it stopped working?
- Is the problem on this computer only or others too?
- What error message appears, exactly?

Write it down. In real support work, notes are your power.

2) Build a troubleshooting checklist mindset

For common issues, create simple checklists.

Examples:

No internet:

- Check network icon
- Check connection status
- Restart adapter
- Run troubleshoot
- Check proxy settings
- Restart router if needed

No sound:

- Check volume and mute
- Check default playback device
- Check if device is disabled
- Restart computer
- Only then consider drivers

Printer not printing:

- Check power/paper/jam
- Check default printer
- Check offline/paused
- Clear queue
- Print test page
- Only then reinstall

This is how professionals stay calm while others panic.

3) Learn Device Manager basics (carefully)

Device Manager is where you see hardware devices and driver status.

As a beginner moving toward IT:

- Learn how to identify devices with warning icons.
- Learn how to view driver details.

- Learn how to disable and re-enable a device safely.

Do not start by updating drivers randomly. Start by observing and understanding.

4) Learn basic networking concepts

You do not need deep networking at first, but you should understand:

- IP address, gateway, DNS (basic meaning)
- Difference between Wi-Fi and router and ISP
- How to tell if it is a device problem or network-wide problem

This knowledge makes you valuable quickly.

5) Practice using a virtual machine for safe experiments

If you can, set up a virtual Windows environment to practice without risking your real computer.

In a virtual machine, you can safely practice:

- Installing and uninstalling programs
- Changing settings
- Triggering StickyKeys and fixing it
- Messing up file associations and restoring them
- Changing region formats and undoing

- Testing printer workflows (virtual printers can still teach the process)

The benefit is confidence. When you practice safely, you become less afraid of breaking things.

6) Learn documentation and communication

Junior support work is not only technical. It is communication.

Practice writing short, clear notes like:

- Issue: User cannot print.
- Findings: Printer set to offline. Queue had stuck jobs.
- Action: Turned off "Use Printer Offline," cleared queue, printed test page successfully.
- Result: Printing restored.

This makes you professional and trustworthy.

7) Learn the difference between fix and prevention

A real technician does not only fix today's problem. They reduce the chance of tomorrow's problem.

Prevention habits you learned in this book are the foundation:

- Standard accounts for daily work
- Show file extensions

- Safe AutoPlay settings
- Minimal startup clutter
- Weekly backups
- Calm update checks
- Documentation of changes

When you help someone, teach them one prevention habit, not ten. Small changes stick.

A final "safe habits" checklist to carry forward

Keep these habits as your personal rules:

- Change one thing at a time.
- Test after every change.
- Keep notes so you can undo.
- Use standard accounts for daily work.
- Be cautious with unknown downloads and installers.
- Show file extensions.
- Keep sharing off on public networks.
- Use official tools for uninstalling programs.
- Back up important files regularly.
- Restart when troubleshooting stalls.

- Do not use aggressive "cleaner" tools that promise miracles.

These habits will keep a Windows 7 computer stable, and they will also serve you on Windows 10, Windows 11, or any future system.

Where to go from here

You now have a strong beginner foundation. Your next steps depend on your goal.

If your goal is personal confidence:

- Keep using the weekly routine.
- Apply the safety habits.
- Help one family member troubleshoot calmly.

If your goal is IT support:

- Practice on a virtual machine.
- Learn Device Manager and basic networking.
- Start documenting real problems and fixes.
- Volunteer to support a small group of users and learn from patterns.

If your goal is junior admin work:

- Study user accounts, permissions, backups, and update policies more deeply.
- Learn how to manage multiple computers consistently.

- Learn how to communicate with users and set safe boundaries.

Windows 7 may be older, but the skills you learned here are not old. They are foundational. Good troubleshooting, safe habits, and clear thinking never expire.

END OF BOOK

You have finished the main content. In the next section (appendix material), you can keep quick checklists and cheat sheets you can print and keep near your computer, so you can troubleshoot without searching online every time.

APPENDIX A: QUICK MAP OF CONTROL PANEL

This appendix is designed to be a fast "where do I go?" guide. You will see two views:

1. Category View map (how beginners usually see it)

2. Icon View map (Large icons or Small icons, how many technicians prefer to see it)

Use this map when you feel stuck, or when you want to jump straight to the right tool without guessing.

A1) Category View map (the beginner-friendly map)

System and Security

Go here when the problem is about system health, protection, updates, power, or backups.

Common tools you will find here:

- Action Center (security and maintenance alerts)

- Windows Firewall (allowing apps, basic protection)

- Windows Update (update settings and history)

- System (system info, device name, performance basics)

- System Protection (restore points)
- Power Options (sleep, hibernate, power plans)
- Backup and Restore (basic backups)
- Administrative Tools (advanced tools, be careful)

Common reasons to open this category:

- "Windows says I have security warnings."
- "A program can't connect to the internet."
- "I want to check update settings."
- "I need a restore point."
- "My laptop sleeps too fast."
- "I want to back up my files."

Network and Internet

Go here when the problem is about internet access, network sharing, and browser internet settings.

Common tools you will find here:

- Network and Sharing Center (connectivity status, network type)
- Change adapter settings (network adapters)
- HomeGroup (sharing in home networks, can confuse beginners)

- Internet Options (browser privacy and security settings)
- Remote Desktop and remote settings (in some setups)

Common reasons to open this category:

- "No internet."
- "Wi-Fi is connected but nothing loads."
- "I need to change sharing settings."
- "My network is set to Public but it should be Home or Work."
- "Internet settings feel wrong or too restrictive."

Hardware and Sound

Go here when the problem is about printers, devices, audio, AutoPlay, or driver-linked behavior.

Common tools you will find here:

- Devices and Printers (printers and device status)
- Device Manager (drivers and hardware status)
- Sound (playback and recording devices, default device)
- AutoPlay (USB and media behavior)
- Power Options (also appears here)

Common reasons to open this category:

- "Printer won't print."
- "No sound."
- "Headphones not working."
- "USB drive opens something weird."
- "I need to add a printer."

Programs

Go here when the problem is about installed software, uninstalling properly, repairs, defaults, and file associations.

Common tools you will find here:

- Programs and Features (uninstall, change, repair)
- Default Programs (default apps, file type associations)
- Desktop Gadgets (Windows 7 gadgets, be cautious)

Common reasons to open this category:

- "I need to uninstall something."
- "A program is broken and needs repair."
- "A file opens in the wrong program."
- "A new program took over my PDFs or photos."

- "My desktop gadgets are acting strange."

User Accounts and Family Safety

Go here when the problem is about accounts, passwords, shared computers, and parental limits.

Common tools you will find here:

- User Accounts (change password, account type)
- Manage another account (admin tasks)
- Parental Controls (time limits, game and program limits)

Common reasons to open this category:

- "I need a new user account."
- "I forgot a password."
- "Who has admin rights?"
- "I want to set limits for kids."
- "I want separate accounts for family members."

Appearance and Personalization

Go here when the problem is about the desktop, taskbar, readability, display comfort, fonts, and how files appear.

Common tools you will find here:

- Personalization (themes, backgrounds, sounds, screen saver)

- Taskbar and Start Menu (taskbar settings, notification area)
- Display (text size, resolution basics via links)
- Fonts (installed fonts)
- Folder Options (file extensions, hidden files)

Common reasons to open this category:

- "Text is too small."
- "Screen looks blurry or stretched."
- "My taskbar is full of clutter."
- "My files look weird, extensions are hidden."
- "I can't find files I know exist."

Clock, Region, and Language

Go here when the problem is about time, time zones, date formats, number formats, and keyboard layouts.

Common tools you will find here:

- Date and Time (time zone, extra clocks, time sync)
- Region and Language (formats, keyboard layouts)

Common reasons to open this category:

- "My time is wrong."
- "Websites show certificate errors."
- "Dates are confusing."
- "Numbers use commas instead of dots."
- "Keyboard types wrong symbols."

Ease of Access

Go here when the problem is about accessibility tools, reading and hearing support, keyboard and mouse help, or accidental StickyKeys.

Common tools you will find here:

- Ease of Access Center (Magnifier, Narrator, High Contrast)
- Keyboard and mouse ease settings
- Speech Recognition (when available)

Common reasons to open this category:

- "Screen is zoomed and I can't fix it."
- "High Contrast turned on and the screen looks strange."
- "StickyKeys is on."
- "Mouse stopped working, need keyboard help."
- "I want Magnifier or Speech Recognition."

A2) Icon View map (Large icons or Small icons)

Icon view lists tools directly. Here are the most important ones from this book, grouped by what they affect.

Security, Updates, Maintenance

- Action Center
- Windows Firewall
- Windows Update
- System
- Backup and Restore
- Power Options
- Administrative Tools

Networks and Internet

- Network and Sharing Center
- Internet Options

Hardware, Printers, Audio

- Devices and Printers
- Device Manager
- Sound
- AutoPlay

Programs and Defaults

- Programs and Features
- Default Programs
- Desktop Gadgets

Accounts and Safety

- User Accounts
- Parental Controls (if present)

Display and File Viewing Habits

- Personalization
- Taskbar and Start Menu
- Display
- Folder Options
- Fonts

Time, Formats, Typing

- Date and Time
- Region and Language

Accessibility Tools

- Ease of Access Center
- Speech Recognition (if present)

Tip:
If you become comfortable with icon view, troubleshooting becomes faster because you do not have to guess the category.

APPENDIX B: COMMON FIXES CHECKLIST

These checklists are short on purpose. They are meant to be used quickly. The order matters. Start at the top and move down. Do not jump to advanced steps first.

B1) "No internet" checklist

1. Check the network icon in the taskbar.
2. Confirm Wi-Fi is connected (or cable is plugged in).
3. Restart the browser and try one trusted website.
4. Restart the computer.
5. Open Network and Sharing Center and check:
    - Does it show connected or disconnected?
    - What network type is it using (Home, Work, Public)?
6. If Wi-Fi:
    - Disconnect and reconnect to the network.
    - Try forgetting and re-entering the password if needed (if you know it).

7. If cable:

    o Try a different cable or port.

8. Check Windows Firewall only if a specific app cannot connect (not when all internet is down).

9. If other devices in the building also have no internet, the issue may be router or ISP, not your PC.

10. If the issue started after new software, consider uninstalling the recent program.

Stop and escalate if:

- It is a work computer with company network rules.

- You see repeated security warnings or strange pop-ups.

- You suspect malware.

B2) "No sound" checklist

1. Check the speaker icon: not muted, volume up.

2. Confirm speakers or headphones are plugged in and powered.

3. Open Control Panel > Hardware and Sound > Sound.

4. Playback tab:

    o Identify the correct device.

- Set it as Default.

5. If you use HDMI or a monitor:

    - Make sure Windows is not sending audio to the monitor by mistake.

6. Right-click inside the Playback list:

    - Show Disabled Devices
    - Enable your speakers if disabled

7. Test sound.

8. Restart the computer.

9. Only then consider driver issues (Device Manager) if the sound device shows errors.

Stop and escalate if:

- Audio device is missing entirely.
- Device Manager shows driver errors and you are not comfortable with drivers.

B3) "Printer not printing" checklist

1. Check printer power and paper.
2. Check printer screen for errors or paper jams.
3. Confirm correct printer is selected as Default.
4. Open Devices and Printers.
5. Open the printer queue:

- Cancel stuck jobs
6. Printer menu:
    - Make sure "Use Printer Offline" is not checked
    - Make sure "Pause Printing" is not checked
7. Print a test page from Printer properties.
8. Restart printer, then restart computer.
9. If network printer:
    - Confirm the PC is on the correct network.
    - Confirm others can print (if possible).
10. Only reinstall drivers if the test page fails repeatedly and basic checks did not help.

Stop and escalate if:

- This is an office printer managed by IT.
- You do not have permission to change drivers.
- Printer hardware error is shown on the printer itself.

B4) "Slow PC" checklist

1. Restart the computer (simple and often effective).

2. Check free disk space on C: drive.

3. Uninstall programs you truly do not use (Programs and Features).

4. Check for a recently installed program that matches when slowdown began (sort by Installed On).

5. Reduce taskbar and notification clutter (less background noise helps).

6. Run a trusted malware scan if behavior is suspicious.

7. Avoid "PC cleaner" and "registry cleaner" tools that promise miracles.

8. If the PC is still slow, the system may need hardware upgrades (more RAM, SSD) or professional servicing.

Stop and escalate if:

- The PC is part of a company environment.
- The slowdown is sudden and accompanied by pop-ups, redirects, or unknown programs.

B5) "Wrong default program" checklist

1. Identify the file type (example: .pdf, .jpg, .mp3).

2. Open Control Panel > Programs > Default Programs.

3. Choose:

- Set your default programs (for broad changes), or
- Associate a file type with a program (for one file type)

4. Select the correct program.
5. Test by double-clicking a file.
6. If the correct program is not available, install a trusted program first, then set it as default.

Stop and escalate if:

- The file type is associated with a suspicious unknown program.
- You suspect malware changed associations.

APPENDIX C: GLOSSARY (BEGINNER-FRIENDLY DEFINITIONS)

This glossary uses plain language. It is here so you can quickly understand terms used throughout the book.

Account
A user profile on Windows. Each account has its own files and settings.

Administrator (Admin)
A powerful account type that can install programs and change system-wide settings.

AutoPlay
A feature that decides what Windows does when you insert a USB drive, CD, or memory card.

Backup
A copy of your important files stored somewhere else so you can recover them if the computer fails.

Browser
A program used to visit websites, such as Internet Explorer or other browsers.

Category View
The Control Panel view that groups settings into categories like System and Security.

Certificate (Website certificate)
A security proof used by secure websites. Wrong system time can cause certificate warnings.

Clock Drift
When the computer time slowly becomes wrong over days or weeks.

Control Panel
A Windows tool that lets you view and change system settings.

Default Program
The program Windows uses automatically to open a file type.

Device
Hardware connected to your computer, such as a printer, mouse, keyboard, or speakers.

Device Driver (Driver)
Software that helps Windows talk to a hardware device.

Device Manager
A tool that lists hardware devices and shows driver status.

Disk Space
How much storage is available on the hard drive.

Display Resolution
How sharp and detailed the screen looks, based on pixel settings.

Extensions (File extensions)
The letters after a dot in a filename, like .pdf or .jpg. They show the file type.

Firewall
A security feature that controls which connections are allowed in and out of the computer.

Folder Options
Settings that control how folders and files appear, including hidden files and file extensions.

Format (Date/Number format)
The style used to display dates, times, and numbers, which can vary by region.

Guest Account
A limited account meant for temporary use by visitors.

High Contrast
A display mode that makes text and screen elements easier to see with strong color contrast.

Icon View
The Control Panel view that lists settings as individual icons, not grouped by category.

Input Language
A setting that controls language behavior for typing and sometimes spelling tools.

Keyboard Layout
A setting that decides what characters your keys type.

Magnifier
A tool that zooms the screen to make text and objects easier to see.

Narrator
A basic screen reader that reads text and UI elements aloud.

Notification Area (System tray)
The area near the clock that shows small icons for background programs and system status.

Parental Controls
Windows settings that can limit time, games, and programs for a child account.

Power Plan
A set of settings that controls how the computer uses power, sleep, and performance.

Programs and Features
The Control Panel tool used to uninstall, change, or repair installed programs.

Restore Point
A saved system state that can help undo certain system changes if something goes wrong.

Standard User
A safer account type for daily work. It cannot easily make system-wide changes without admin approval.

StickyKeys
An accessibility feature that lets you press modifier keys one at a time instead of holding them down.

Taskbar
The bar at the bottom of the screen that shows the Start button, open programs, and system icons.

Time Zone
A region-based time setting. Wrong time zone causes the clock to be off by hours.

UAC (User Account Control)
Windows prompts that ask for permission before system-level changes are made.

Windows Update
A Windows feature that installs updates and fixes for the system.

If you want, the next appendices can be quick one-page "cheat sheets" you can print: one for network, one for printers, one for audio, and one for file safety (extensions and hidden files).

FINAL NOTE TO THE READER

You made it to the end, and that matters.

Most people use Windows for years and still feel nervous the moment something goes wrong. They click around, they guess, and they hope the problem disappears. That is not a skill. That is stress.

If you followed this book in order, you now have something better than random confidence. You have habits.

You can find the right settings without panic.
You can change one thing at a time and test.
You can write down changes so you can reverse them.
You can keep your computer usable with simple weekly maintenance.
You can help someone else without breaking their system.

That is what real computer literacy looks like.

Windows 7 may be older, but the discipline you learned here is timeless. Every version of Windows still has the same truth underneath: the system is manageable when you approach it calmly, and it becomes chaos when you treat it like a mystery box.

Keep your habits simple:

- Change one thing at a time.

- Test immediately.

- Keep notes.
- Avoid unknown downloads.
- Back up what matters.

If you do that, you will stay ahead of most problems.

Quick Maintenance Routine

This is the short version you can print or keep near your desk.

Weekly (15 to 30 minutes)

1. Restart the computer.
2. Check the time and date are correct.
3. Check Windows Update status (if your system uses it).
4. Check free space on C: drive.
5. Back up important folders (Documents, Desktop, Pictures).
6. Open the browser and confirm one trusted website loads.
7. If you print often, print a quick test page.

Monthly (30 to 60 minutes)

1. Review installed programs (Programs and Features, sort by Installed On).
2. Remove programs you truly do not use (uninstall properly).

3. Confirm accounts and admin rights are still correct.

4. Confirm backups can restore one file successfully.

5. Review the taskbar notification area and remove clutter.

Anytime something feels wrong

1. Ask: did anything change recently?

2. Undo the last change you made, if possible.

3. Test again before changing something else.

4. If the issue is bigger than your comfort level, stop and get help early.

Quick Safety Rules to Keep

1. Use a Standard account for daily work.

2. Use an Admin account only when you must install or change system-wide settings.

3. Keep file extensions visible.

4. Keep AutoPlay set to safe options.

5. Do not install unknown fonts, gadgets, or "helper" toolbars.

6. Do not use aggressive "cleaner" or "registry repair" tools.

7. Back up first before big changes.

Troubleshooting Log Template

Use this page when you are fixing a problem. It turns stress into a clear process.

Problem Report

- Date:
- Computer name (if known):
- User:
- Problem description (exact words the user said):
- When did it start?
- What changed before it started (new program, update, device, network, account change)?
- Is it happening for one program or for everything?

Checks Done

- Time and date correct? Yes / No
- Network connected? Yes / No
- Disk space low? Yes / No
- Any warnings in Action Center? Yes / No
- Any unusual pop-ups? Yes / No

Actions Taken (one change at a time)

1. Change made:

- Where (Control Panel path):
- Why:
- Result:

2. Change made:
   - Where (Control Panel path):
   - Why:
   - Result:

3. Change made:
   - Where (Control Panel path):
   - Why:
   - Result:

Final Outcome

- Problem fixed? Yes / No
- What solved it?
- What should be done to prevent it next time?

Mini Cheat Sheets

If the keyboard suddenly behaves strangely

1. Press Windows key + U to open Ease of Access Center.
2. Check StickyKeys and turn it off.
3. Check FilterKeys and turn it off.

4. Check Mouse Keys and turn it off.

5. Go to Region and Language and confirm the correct keyboard layout is selected.

If secure websites show certificate warnings

1. Check Date and Time.

2. Confirm correct time zone.

3. Correct time and date.

4. If possible, sync with Internet Time.

5. Restart the browser and test again.

If a file opens in the wrong program

1. Open Default Programs.

2. Associate the file type with the correct program.

3. Test by opening the file again.

Next Learning Steps

If you want to grow from confident user to someone who supports others, follow a simple path. Do not rush.

Step 1: Become consistent at the basics

- Control Panel navigation
- Uninstall and defaults
- Network and printer basics

- Sound device selection
- Account types and admin rights
- File extensions and hidden file awareness
- Restore points and basic backups

Step 2: Add two technician skills

1. Device Manager observation
   Learn how to spot warning icons and read device status without changing drivers randomly.

2. Network basics
   Learn the meaning of IP address, gateway, DNS, and how to tell the difference between a device problem and a network problem.

Step 3: Practice safely

If you can, practice inside a test environment (a spare PC or a virtual machine). Practice these tasks:

- Breaking and fixing default programs
- Turning on and off StickyKeys and High Contrast
- Changing region formats and restoring
- Creating and managing accounts
- Testing simple backup and restore

Step 4: Learn to document fixes

Professional support is not only the fix. It is the record of the fix. Use the Troubleshooting Log template until it becomes natural.

Leave a Review

If this book helped you, a short review makes a real difference. It helps other beginners find a guide they can trust.

If you leave a review, you can mention:

- What problem you were trying to solve
- Which chapter helped the most
- What new habit you gained (file extensions, backups, standard accounts, taskbar cleanup)

Thank you for supporting practical learning.

Stay Connected

If you want updates, new guides, or training materials, you can reach the author here:

- Website: www.johnshalom.com
- Email: maluthabiel@gmail.com
- Phone: +211 927 145 394

Permissions, Bulk Orders, and Training Use

If you want to:

- order copies for a school, office, or training program
- request permission for structured training use
- sponsor a local digital literacy program

Contact the author using the details above and include:

- Your organization name
- Country and city
- Number of learners or copies needed
- How the book will be used (classroom, community training, office onboarding)

Other Books and Guides

If you enjoyed this beginner-friendly style, here are good directions for your next learning step:

- Windows file management (folders, search, backups, safe storage)
- Internet safety for beginners (phishing, downloads, passwords)
- Basic networking for home and small office
- Printer and troubleshooting guide for beginners
- Intro to IT support habits (tickets, checklists, documentation)

(If this book is part of a series, list the titles here.)

END

ABOUT THE AUTHOR

John Monyjok Maluth is a South Sudanese writer, teacher, and technology professional who builds practical guides for everyday people. His work focuses on clear language, real-life problem solving, and habits that help beginners become confident users without fear of breaking their computers.

He has worked in ICT and communications roles supporting teams, offices, and community users, and he is known for turning technical topics into simple steps that anyone can follow. His wider writing mission is rooted in inspiration, empowerment, and integrity, with a belief that digital skills are part of modern dignity and opportunity.

Website: www.johnshalom.com
Email: maluthabiel@gmail.com
Phone: +211 927 145 394

www.ingramcontent.com/pod-product-compliance
Lightning Source LLC
Chambersburg PA
CBHW031612210526
45464CB00004B/1541